MORE PRAISE FOR
WAKING UP TOGETHER

"Ellen and Charles Birx have written a wise and lovely book about the fundamental aspects of living a spiritual life together. *Waking Up Together* clearly shows that deep committed relationship and deep committed spiritual practice mutually support each other, like two vines growing intertwined. We wish we had such a spiritually based, compassionate, and broad view to support the beginnings of our relationship over two decades ago. We welcome this charming book. It is certain to be very helpful for couples of all faiths."
Chozen and Hogen Bays, co-abbots,
Great Vow Zen Monastery, Clatskanie, Oregon

"This is no ordinary book on relationships. The wealth of insight Ellen and Charles share is not only grounded in the rich soil of their own long partnership with each other, but illumined from within by deep experience in a spiritual tradition that leads us to the source of all intimacy."
Roshi Bodhin Kjolhede, abbot,
Rochester Zen Center, New York

"This book makes real what has, up to now, been simply given lip service: the non-duality of practice life and relationship life. The psychologically sound recommendations made by the authors can apply to all couples, Buddhist and non-Buddhist alike. It is a rich resource for couples on the path."
Angela Stewart, Ph.D., Clinical Psychologist

WAKING UP TOGETHER

WAKING UP TOGETHER

INTIMATE PARTNERSHIP ON THE SPIRITUAL PATH

Ellen Jikai Birx

Charles Shinkai Birx

WISDOM PUBLICATIONS • BOSTON

Wisdom Publications, Inc.
199 Elm Street
Somerville MA 02144 USA
www.wisdompubs.org

Library of Congress Cataloging-in-Publication Data

Birx, Ellen.
 Waking up together : intimate partnership on the spiritual path / Ellen Jikai Birx, Charles Shinkai Birx.
     p. cm.
  Includes index.
  ISBN 0-86171-395-8 (pbk. : alk. paper)
   I. Interpersonal relations—Religious aspects. 2. Intimacy (Psychology)—Religious aspects. I. Birx, Charles Shinkai. II. Title.
  BL626.33.B57 2005
  294.3'4441—dc22

                                                    2004029381

ISBN 0-86171-395-8
First Edition
09 08 07 06 05
5   4   3   2   1

Cover design by Mary Ann Smith.
Interior design by Gopa&Ted2, Inc. Set in Centaur 12/19 pt.

Wisdom Publications' books are printed on acid-free paper and meet the guidelines for permanence and durability set by the Council of Library Resources.

Printed in the United States of America.

To our teacher
Roshi Robert Jinsen Kennedy

CONTENTS

PREFACE

THIS BOOK is written to encourage those who want to journey to new depths of intimacy both spiritually and in their relationships. *Waking Up Together: Intimate Partnership on the Spiritual Path* shows how a committed, long-term relationship can enhance spiritual development and how relationships can be transformed by spiritual practice.

Although spiritual practice is certainly helpful in meeting the challenges and difficulties often encountered in life and in relationships, many erroneously assume that spiritual insight automatically and effortlessly manifests in healthy, satisfying relationships. Insight, awakening, or realization is just the first step. This book serves as a guide for *actualizing* your spiritual insight, bringing it to life in your primary intimate relationship. We hope to show you how to stay young and new for each other even as you grow old and wise together. Truly, a stable, loving relationship not only enriches your own life but its positive influence extends out to nurture humanity, the earth, and all beings.

The approach we take in this book is informed by our six collective decades of Zen study, practice, and teaching. Zen is a simple but profound approach to meditation and life that emphasizes open clarity of mind and the direct experience of *nonduality*—the intimate experience of life itself, unobscured by thoughts, categories, and concepts. Nonduality is the experience of the extraordinary nature of ordinary life. But although this book is written from a Zen perspective and uses occasional Zen references or terms, it nonetheless sheds universal light on many of the long-standing and tenacious relationship issues we all deal with in some form or other. It is our hope that the ideas, options, and suggestions in this book are useful for couples in any spiritual tradition or none.

Throughout the book we will offer practical, concrete, and psychologically sound suggestions for improving your relationship with your partner. However this book also goes far beyond mere skills and strategies, to show how spiritual insights can transform your relationship and enhance your quality of life at their very roots. And, though we will draw on concepts and ideas from many psychological and family therapy approaches, this book is rooted in nonduality.

Yet we are not suggesting that meditation or nonduality is a panacea for psychological or relationship problems. To the contrary, we encourage people to use all skillful means available to them, including the professional help of psychotherapists, psychiatrists, and marriage and family therapists. But spiritual practice and development also provide valuable resources that open up whole new possibilities for enlivening and empowering relationships.

From a Zen perspective, a relationship is neither perfect nor imperfect. Your relationship is just what it is. The challenge is to appreciate it—whatever it is—moment by moment and to learn from it, whatever it is, moment by moment.

Throughout this book, we have intermingled Zen stories, poems, and traditional teaching stories called *koans* along with stories from our thirty-seven years of married life. This will, we hope, make clear how we integrate the infinite subtlety of Zen with the beauty and challenges of our everyday life together. And yet we are not holding up our relationship as a paragon, but only sharing glimpses of the lives and relationships we know best. Our goal is to show one possible way to be a couple committed to both deep spiritual practice and a long-term, loving relationship, and to help make this useful to you in your relationship.

Writing this book together is a testament to the strength of our relationship and to the spirit of cooperation. It has led to a valuable dialogue that has deepened our connection and brought us closer. Our hope is that this book will inspire other couples to cultivate the richness of their own relationships and open to the unbounded potential for love to blossom.

Ellen and Charles Birx

Radford, Virginia

Spring 2005

ACKNOWLEDGMENTS

WE EXPRESS our deep gratitude to our Zen teacher Roshi Robert Kennedy, his teacher Roshi Bernie Glassman, and all the teachers in our lineage for their wisdom and diligence in keeping this practice alive. Roshi Wendy Egyoko Nakao has been particularly inspiring and supportive of our work. We also thank all the Zen practitioners who have supported our sitting down through the years, especially Russell Ball, Rosemary O'Connell, Miriam Healy, Br. Jeffrey Briggs, Rose and Jim Ramsay, Sr. Johanna Leahy, Jan Hencke, Monica Appleby, and all the members of New River Zen Community.

We express our special appreciation for our daughter, Clare, our son-in-law, Troy, and our three lively grandchildren, Matthew, Brenna, and Elise, for many happy moments during the writing of this book. Appreciation also goes to Ellen's mother, Kathleen Clark, who has always empowered her as a woman.

Warm thanks go to Charles' sister, Carol DeKyid Birx, who has been a special companion on the spiritual path through her committed practice of Tibetan Buddhism.

We are grateful to Ellen's colleagues at Radford University for their support of her Faculty Professional Developmental Leave during the spring 2004 semester that allowed her time to work on this project.

Many thanks go to Josh Bartok, who not only has superb skill as an editor but also a deep understanding of spiritual practice. Through this combination he helped bring focus and clarity to this book.

LIVING IN A SPIRITUAL RELATIONSHIP

AN INTIMATE JOURNEY

DURING THE EARLY YEARS of our marriage we lived in Kaibeto, Arizona, on the Navajo Indian reservation where Charles was a teacher at a Bureau of Indian Affairs boarding school. Often Navajo friends who worked at the school invited us to a *sing* that was taking place at the hogan of a family member. A sing is a healing ceremony that may last several days, and in addition to improving the condition of the patient, it brings the community back into harmony and balance. One evening we drove off across the desert into the night in our forest green Chevy pickup on a barely visible dirt track, following the sound of distant chanting until we arrived at a cluster of pickup trucks and a crackling fire circled with Navajo men, women, and children. We joined the group and listened for several hours to the ancient songs, watching the sprinkling of sacred pollen and breathing the sweet scent of the pinon smoke.

At about midnight a couple in their eighties we didn't recognize came out of the hogan and sat cross-legged on the ground across from us, at the position of honor in the circle. Their long white hair, usually tied in a knot and neatly wrapped with white yarn, was hanging loose over their shoulders to their waists. We were captivated by their magnificent dignity as a couple, and then after about an hour, they got up and left. We never found out who they were, but encountering this couple who had grown so old together was for us quite powerful, almost archetypal, and we carry that image in our hearts to this day.

Thirty years later, we found ourselves in Litchfield, Connecticut, at an intensive Zen meditation retreat called a *sesshin*, held by Roshi Bernie Glassman. We had driven there from our home in Radford, Virginia, during one of the worst winter blizzards we had ever seen. Part of the trip was on back roads since sections of the interstate were closed due to the storm. Our teacher Roshi Robert Kennedy was performing the special "Dharma transmission" ceremony in which we would both become formally authorized to teach Zen.

As we stood side by side during our ceremony performing the fifty-four traditional bows in tandem, we were aware of the fact that this was probably the first time in the history of Zen that a married couple was being transmitted together. It is a relatively recent phenomenon that women are recognized as Zen teachers at all, and now here we were—husband and wife. Later that day as we shared our impressions of the ceremony with each other, we were surprised to discover that old Navajo couple had visited us both.

As Buddhism begins to take root in American soil, many of the people who seek it out are married or in a committed relationship. Historically, however, Zen is largely a monastic tradition. Many people are deeply interested in how to sustain a serious meditation practice and lead a life devoted to spiritual development while at the same time living together as a couple or family and maintaining a career. Ultimately, is the Dharma consistent with a committed life-long relationship, or, like Buddha himself, are those serious about awakening doomed to leave spouse and children behind?

Recently, at a weekend retreat Ellen encountered a poem by Marilou Awiakta that was framed and hanging on the wall by a large stone fireplace. It was about Selu, the Cherokee Corn-Mother, and her husband Lucky Hunter, and it said that they were partners "in life and wisdom." Later that morning, when Ellen entered the meditation hall to give a talk, she looked around the room and realized that everyone there was married or in a committed relationship. How can *zazen*, Zen meditation—a silent practice of sitting alone on a cushion—help couples be partners in both life and in wisdom?

Sometimes Zen seems particularly impersonal, with its silence and rigor and discipline—but Zen is a master at paradox, and what seems cold and distant is also warm and personal. Truly when we practice zazen we sit intimately.

There is a Zen story that helps us appreciate the many levels and facets of intimacy, perhaps the most essential ingredient in fulfilling relationships:

For many years, Liangshan studied with Master Tongan Guanzhi, and served as his attendant. One day as Liangshan handed Tongan his robe, he asked him, "What is the business beneath the patched robe?" At this, Liangshan was greatly awakened and tears of gratitude flowed from his eyes. Tongan asked him if he could express his realization and Liangshan said that he could. So Tongan asked him, "What is the business beneath the patched robe?" Liangshan said, "Intimacy." And Tongan responded, "Intimacy, intimacy."

Sitting in meditation, silent and attentive, you get to know yourself better. You become familiar with the sensations in your body and with the rhythm of your breathing. You see how your mind works—the stories you tell yourself over and over again, the things you worry about, your judgments, wants, needs, and expectations. And you learn about the freedom and energy available if you let go of all that. During meditation you become aware of emotions welling up within, building to some intensity, and then waning—rising and falling like waves in the ocean. You learn how to move with emotions and become less reactive, more equanimous. Getting to know yourself intimately is a necessary foundation of an intimate relationship with anyone else.

If you let go of your judgments, opinions, and preconceived ideas about your partner, you can experience the immediacy of the present moment together, just as it is, full and vibrant.

There is a Zen story about a monk named Fayan who went on a pilgrimage to visit many teachers. One day it rained so hard that it started to flood, so he stopped at a monastery where Zen Master Guichen lived. Guichen asked Fayan, "Where are you going and for what reason?" Fayan replied, "I don't know." Guichen said, "Not knowing is most intimate."

Often in life and in relationships we don't know where we are going, and we don't know for what reason. We don't know what will happen next or how long something will last. Sometimes we think we know our partner so well that he or she is entirely predictable, yet even then if you let go of your predictions and expectations, you will discover there is much about your partner that you do *not* know—and you regain the marvelous capacity to be surprised. Not knowing is the mystery and wonder in life. Not knowing is most intimate.

In addition to intimacy with yourself and intimacy in relationships, Zen practice helps you take a leap into an even deeper experience of intimacy, closing the gap between self and other completely, directly experiencing nonseparation. There is no subject or object, no I or Thou nor me or you, no separate self at all. In your essential nature you are one with the entire universe. There is no distance between your light and the light of the farthest star. Paradoxically, this direct experience of oneness supports the differentiation that enables you to stand on your own two feet as an individual while entering into the intimacy of a shared relationship. When Buddha sat down in meditation beneath the Bodhi Tree his enlightenment was triggered by seeing the morning star, and at that moment he exclaimed, "How wonderful, how marvelous! I and the great earth and all beings simultaneously achieve the Way." He woke up and experienced the intimate unity of all creation.

In one sense we journey alone, but in another we wake up together.

EXPANDING YOUR HEART

THERE IS A ZEN VERSE that says, "The deep, subtle secret must not be lodged in a one-inch heart." Here the "deep, subtle secret" refers to enlightenment, but we can also read it as intimacy in relationship. For loving relationships to flourish we must expand our hearts and our capacity to love. Though there is a miraculous fist-sized muscle in your chest efficiently pumping blood night and day, your heart is not confined within your rib cage.

When you sit in Zen meditation, every cell in your body is awake and alert. You become clear and sensitive and hear not just with your ears. You feel a cricket's chirping ripple through your entire body. In the crisp morning air, a birdsong calls out to the ends of the earth. Love sings. In the deep silence and subtle stillness of sitting, you experience that mind too is boundless—not limited to space inside your head. Mind and heart extend throughout your body and throughout the universe.

Zen Master Dogen, one of the great spiritual thinkers of all time, wrote a piece called *Bendowa*, "The Wholehearted Way." He says, "The wholehearted practice of the Way that I am talking about allows all things to exist in enlightenment and enables us to live out oneness in the path of emancipation." The wholehearted way is a life lived with heart wide open. It is the direct experience of the vast unboundedness of your heart. Relationships that nurture, liberate, and last require this wholeheartedness of love.

Without an expanded heart, relationships become clinging and suffocating rather than enlivening. What we like today may become tomorrow's irritation. What we agree on today may become tomorrow's disagreement. Relationships limited to the narrow constraints of our likes and dislikes imprison us. But don't get us wrong: having likes and dislikes is to be expected, and it is important you know them intimately, but it is vital that you not be bound by them. You are more than your likes and dislikes!

All of us need to be free to change and grow, and the challenge in relationship is to learn how to move along together. Love is not something you have or don't have. It is not a possession. It is what you are. You must be able to experience that which is beyond likes and dislikes, beyond agreeing and disagreeing, beyond have and have not, and beyond clinging to cherished memories of what your relationship was like in the past and expectations of what it should be in the future. Experience a life that is expansive, inclusive, and open to what is. This is the meaning of the wholehearted way.

Another Zen story that may be illuminating here:

One day Zen Master Xuefeng addressed the assembly of monks, saying, "All the great world, if I pick it up with my fingertips, is found to be like a grain of rice. I throw it in front of your face, but you do not see it. Beat the drum telling the monks to come out to work, and search for it."

Each person, each leaf, each grain of rice, and each heartbeat contains the whole universe. Yet if you search the whole world over looking for intimacy, for love, you search in vain. The only place you will ever find it is right here. It is your own essential nature and it is the essential nature of the whole world. The beat of the drum is your own heartbeat, and love is as close as that.

One spring, when we both were teaching at a weeklong Zen retreat at a monastery high up in the mountains of Colorado, the sagebrush-covered slopes were abloom with lupine, Indian paintbrush, and mountain bluebells. The normally arid land was being watered by snow that was rapidly melting under the sun blazing in the clear blue sky. This is a good metaphor for how meditation nourishes relationships. With regular meditation practice, the walls we erect around ourselves dissolve in the light of our open attention. When the walls come down, new energy, vitality, and love flow in bringing the relationship back to life, allowing it to flower and grow.

The other day our four-year-old granddaughter stood in the middle of the kitchen while we were cooking dinner and confidently announced, "I love everyone in the whole wide world." Loving everyone in the whole world is embodied in our love for those closest to us and in compassionate action to care for those in need. This is done one grain of rice at a time—one smile, one touch, or one step at a time. The realization and clear vision of the whole universe contained within each small act expands the heart and enables love to bloom right here and now.

BEING A COMPANION

W E ARE NOT separate and isolated beings. All of us have a basic need for companionship and support. We live and grow in relationship with the earth, with animals, and with other people. And most of us want a special relationship with a life partner who is our friend and lover.

A fulfilling long-term relationship is rooted in friendship. Friends genuinely like one another, enjoy each other's company, and have fun together. There is mutual attraction, affection, and warmth. Friends share common interests and activities. They joke and laugh together. They talk with each other about what's happening in the world and in their lives.

As a partnership deepens, a sense of commitment and loyalty develop. You do not hesitate to come to the aid of your partner. You count on your partner to "be there" for you in good times, bad times, and ordinary times too. Over time, a wealth of shared experience fortifies the relationship.

As a couple, often we go down to the state park near our home and walk the deer trail together. We hike up the hill and into the woods in silence, so we don't scare away the deer. Then we silently walk along enjoying the ethereal growth of pine seedlings glistening in the sunlight that filters through the tall trees overhead. We smell the dry leaves and pine needles beneath our feet and notice white, orange, and yellow mushrooms sprouting up here and there along the trail. Suddenly, the deer appear up ahead! We stand like statues and watch as they make their way through the trees, fleeing our intrusion into their private world. When they have gone their way, we begin conversing as we hike on through the forest. It's wonderful to have a lifelong companion with whom you can share familiar rituals such as this.

Part of the process of being partners is finding out about the other person and revealing who you are. At the same time, your partner is like a mirror reflecting back aspects of yourself you hadn't seen before, and in this relationship you learn more fully about who you are. Your partner also learns more about who he or she is and is invited to reveal this to you. Partners come to know each other. They know what they like to eat, what movies or music they enjoy, their opinions on many topics, where they came from, and where they want to go. The process of revealing and receiving involves trust, openness, and honesty. Your partner accepts you, listens to you, and cares how you feel. Partnership is a place of familiarity, comfort, and safety. You can let down your defenses and feel free to be who you are.

A life partner is more than a friend. He or she is the one you choose to be physically intimate with, and to spend the rest of your life with. However, going beyond friendship does not mean that this aspect of your relationship is left behind when you become lovers and life partners. Friendship is the foundation of an intimate relationship and it needs to be continuously nurtured and enjoyed.

In entering into a lifetime partnership, you make a commitment and accept responsibility for supporting the well-being of your partner—and we suggest that this includes a commitment to support the spiritual development of your partner. In order to fulfill this responsibility, you need to make a commitment to your own spiritual development. You can't share what you don't have! You become fellow pilgrims on the way, helping each other along as you journey through life together. Each of you gives the other the freedom and space to find what is meaningful and enlivening at each stage in your life. You are spiritual companions, walking the path together.

There is a Zen koan that asks, "How would you walk straight through a narrow mountain path of forty-nine curves?" We can take this as fair warning. Even though your path is straight in the sense of having your eyes steadfastly on doing what is best for your own and your partner's spiritual development, many unexpected and difficult circumstances are likely to arise, so you need to be very flexible. Don't expect the spiritual path to be straight, smooth, or easy. Be companions that encourage and help one another along.

Meditation practice can help us look deeply into what it means to be a companion. There is a story about a monk named Dongshan who was studying in a monastery headed by Master Nanquan. One day as they were preparing for a memorial service in honor of Zen ancestor Mazu's death, Nanquan said to the monks, "Tomorrow we are going to provide offerings to Mazu—but do you think that he will come?" The monks were silent except for Dongshan who said, "If he has a companion, he will come." Nanquan praised this answer.

This story points toward the direct experience of your own essential nature, which is one with the essential nature of Mazu. If you meditate and see this clearly, you experience the quality of attention that is required to be a true companion. You experience that deep down you are not a separate self. You experience oneness and connection with everything and everyone else.

You then need to live out this insight in the relative world, in the particular relationships and circumstances of your life as they arise moment by moment. How can you be a true companion to your partner? This can only be done one day at a time, one step at a time, one moment at a time, but it helps immensely to bring the spirit of being a true companion to your life and relationship. The spirit of true companionship is presence, connection, and an awareness of oneness. The wisdom of true companionship will be an aid on the journey, but it takes ongoing effort and attention to bring this to life, to manifest companionship, to manifest love.

In the Buddhist world, you are encouraged to take refuge in the Buddha, the Dharma, and the Sangha. Taking refuge in the Buddha inspires you to develop your human potential and spiritual insight, and to see for yourself the oneness that Buddha experienced. Taking refuge in the Dharma encourages you to experience vast, unbounded clarity and nonduality in everyday life. Taking refuge in the sangha, you live out your spiritual insights and wisdom in your relationships with others.

Our Zen teacher, Roshi Kennedy, often says to his students, to "Find someone you love and put your arms around them. Take refuge in their love." And when you do, ask yourself, "In whose love do I take refuge?" Don't be too quick to answer, "Well, my partner's of course." Take the time to look deeply into this matter and see that your partner is not other than Buddha, Dharma, and Sangha.

Often at the conclusion of a meditation retreat our days of silence end with a meal and celebration. We have a great time talking with old friends and meeting people we haven't met before. It's always fascinating to chat with a person you have been sitting beside during a week of silent meditation. You know her only by her feet, breathing, and posture, and now you hear her voice and a bit of her story. Often our thoughts stray in meditation and we find ourselves making up stories about the people sitting around us. These stories are shattered in an instant when the woman who looked like a stern librarian turns out to be a social worker with a terrific sense of humor and the man who we imagined was the perfect monk turns out to be married with three lively young children. We also enjoy meeting the husbands, wives, families, and friends who come to pick up the meditators at the end of the retreat.

On one such occasion a man named Dave, who has been mediating with us for many years, was joined by his wife, Deb, and young daughter, Autumn Rose. As we began dinner, he introduced them to the group as "my little sangha." He explained that they do not have a Zen group in their area, so his family is his sangha.

Many people think only of their meditation group as their *true* sangha and as a result sometimes spend a disproportionate amount of time and energy absorbed in sangha activities and matters. Partners can be relegated to second place. This can be brought back into balance and important insights can be gained when we think of our partner and family as our primary sangha. They provide a refuge for us and we for them. As companions, we provide safety, encouragement, and support for one another. We promote the spiritual practice and development of one another and manifest the wisdom we gain in our primary relationships.

These days, many relationships don't last and many even doubt that a fulfilling and lasting relationship is possible. The cynical may wonder if it's possible that love may last a lifetime. Our experience is that love can last—if it has a companion. Daily meditation practice coupled with open attentiveness to your partner yield a deep sense of connection. And this connection is the beginning of learning how to love each other more and more fully.

PARTNER AS TEACHER

ELLEN'S FATHER was a rock collector. Whenever the family went on a vacation, he returned with a burlap bag with an assortment of rocks and crystals of all sizes and descriptions. He put many of the stones into his rock polisher and for days the small silver cylinder would turn round and round. The stones tumbled against each other over and over, and when he took them out they were smooth and shiny and beautiful.

When we live in any community we bump up against each other and eventually it wears down some of the rough edges of our character. This especially happens in our closest relationship, our "littlest sangha," living together day in and day out. We knock against each other continually over big things and little things.

In our relationship, Charles likes to throw old flowers, banana peels, and apple cores off the back deck. He says they're biodegradable and he likes returning them directly to the earth. Ellen prefers to put them in the trash. This is an example of a little difference, and it may even seem trivial. But small differences such as this come up over and over when you are living with a partner, and if you don't take a look at your reaction to them, little aggravations build up and greatly add to the stress in a relationship.

Big issues and differences also arise over the years of a long-term relationship. For example, in our relationship, Charles wanted to have no children and Ellen wanted two. As a result, we have one child. However, much more than compromise is involved in a partnership surviving such a major difference. Each partner needs to hear, understand, and acknowledge what is important to the other.

Both partners need to see if there is a way for each to respect and meet the needs of the other without giving up who each is as an individual. Each partner grows through this kind of soul-searching process and learns more about both self and partner.

There is a well-known Zen story related to this theme of polishing. Mazu practiced zazen diligently every day. One day his teacher, Huairang, came to him and asked, "Worthy one, what are you trying to attain by sitting?" Mazu replied, "I am trying to become a buddha." At this Huairang picked up a roof tile and began polishing it. Mazu asked him, "What are you doing, Master?" Huairang replied, "I am polishing it to make a mirror." Mazu said, "How could polishing a tile make a mirror?" Huairang said, "How could sitting in zazen make a buddha?"

This koan is not suggesting that there is no need to meditate or no need to actively work at a relationship. It is not suggesting that we have no need for polishing. But it is helping us see that there is no need for you (or your partner!) to become "Buddha"—or anyone else, for that matter. When you allow your rough edges, your desire to control, your desire to be right, your self-centered view of the world, to fall away, you become who you truly are. You become more fully your own unique self. Both meditation and relationship are powerful opportunities to learn about who you are and to act accordingly.

Zen meditation is an emptying process. Sitting in silence you let go of thoughts, concepts, and images. When you realize you need not cling to and protect your opinions you can also realize that you needn't strive to maintain any "self-image." You directly experience who you naturally are when all of the excess baggage is laid down. Like meditation practice, an intimate relationship can let you feel safe to let down your guard in a similar fashion. Both figuratively and literally, you are free to be naked with your partner. With your partner you have the greatest opportunity to put into action the insights gained in silence. In this sense, your partner is your teacher who enables you to manifest your deepest insights in your closest relationship.

It takes ongoing work and awareness for this level of trust to develop in a relationship. Partners need to make a conscious effort to let down their defenses and reveal to the other what they are discovering about themselves day by day. Each partner must listen to the other and receive what the other is revealing with an open mind and heart. This doesn't happen all at once. It develops over time with daily practice.

One Zen insight is to experience the natural beauty of your own "original face" and to live out the sheer beauty of being a human being. In beginning to do this, you gain a new appreciation for your own precious life just as it is. You also see the natural beauty of your partner's original face, your partner's larger Self, and the sheer beauty of another unique human being. There is a Navajo song we learned when we lived on the reservation that goes like this:

> *I walk in beauty. Yes I do. Yes I do.*
> *I talk in beauty. Yes I do. Yes I do.*

I sing of beauty. Just for you and only you.
Hey yah hey yah hee yo.

This song can be sung to both the Great Spirit (or the Absolute) and to your own particular lover. Zen urges you to discover in yourself and in the arms of your lover the beauty of relationship.

Seeing your partner as your teacher involves an attitude of reverence, fully realizing the sacred nature of your relationship. Zen Master Dogen tells us that "To study the Buddha Way is to study the self. To study the self is to forget the self. To forget the self is to be enlightened by the myriad things." You are enlightened by everything in the universe—including your partner. A partner shows you where you are stuck, and the resulting friction can help you learn how to move on.

Most of us are stuck in our own self-centered view of the world. For example, often the two of us are on our way home and remember that we are out of, for instance, milk. I (Charles) will pull up in front of the grocery store and Ellen will run in to get the milk. As she heads toward the dairy section, she passes the bread and remembers we need some so she picks up a loaf. Then she remembers that we need dish detergent, and several other items. Fifteen minutes later when she emerges from the store with a whole bag of groceries I give an exasperated sigh and head home feeling irritated—because I was left waiting in the car for minutes on end! This is a clear lesson for me that I am stuck in my own self-centered time frame. The same person who can sit patiently and silently in meditation for hours on end becomes irritated with even a fifteen-minute delay as necessities are attended to? The same is true for Ellen, who becomes very irritated when I decide to shave or take a shower at the last minute before heading out the door to a party. The exact time we arrive at the party seldom makes a difference. Both these situations are an opportunity to look at the feeling of irritation as it arises and the accompanying thoughts that fuel the flame. These occurrences are a time for spiritual practice as important as the time you spend on the meditation cushion!

YOUR PARTNER IS LIKE A SACRED MIRROR held up before you. In it you can see both shadow and light. You can see yourself just as you are. This can inspire both self-acceptance and the motivation to change. When you are having difficulties, your relationship may not seem sacred. A difficult relationship may seem like the greatest cause of suffering in one's life. Buddhism has much to say about suffering—first and foremost the simple fact that it exists. Sometimes just naming and acknowledging the pain you are experiencing brings some relief. It is extremely painful when a special relationship you hoped would bring you happiness in life turns into a source of anguish. Naming and acknowledging the pain brings it out into the light where it can be examined. The sacred includes the whole of life, both the happy and sad times, the good and the bad, relationships that are difficult as well as those that are going well. In all circumstances we can learn and grow. Buddhism also helps us see how selfish desires or clinging cause suffering. In a relationship you quickly learn that you can't always get what you want, since two people's desires have to be taken into account. If you are selfish and cling to having things your way all the time there are sure to be problems in the relationship. Sometimes it is our unrealistic expectations or our desire to control that causes suffering in a relationship. You may expect that you and your partner will enjoy the same activities and friends. However, your partner may want to take up a new activity, say, mountain climbing, in which you have no interest. Yet if you try to control your partner and not allow him or her time to pursue a new interest then your partner, the relationship, and you yourself will suffer. Rather than trying to control your partner, look for something interesting to do by yourself or with friends while your partner is off climbing. When we gain insight into our expectations and desire to control, these can be modified and suffering relieved. We can adjust our expectation that we will always enjoy the same things and that we will do everything together and let go of our attempts to control. Sometimes it is not what happens in a relationship, but our *interpretation* of what happens, that causes us to suffer.

If you interpret your partner's desire to go mountain climbing as an expression of his or her desire to get away from you or as an indication that you are growing apart, you can turn your partner's new interest into a source of suffering. When you stay with what is happening, and do not distort it with interpretation, you do not create problems or exacerbate the pain of a situation.

WE NOT ONLY LEARN FROM EACH OTHER as husband and wife but also learn from each other as Zen teachers. We alternate weeks giving the talk at the Wednesday evening sitting of New River Zen Community. We learn from the talks given by the other because each person has his or her own unique experience and expression of Zen and of life. Even for two people living together all the time, there are two very distinct and different flavors. While we drive home in the dark after the meeting we comment and question each other about the evening's talk and converse about related issues and experiences.

One Wednesday evening I (Charles) gave a talk to New River Zen Community at the end of our sitting. I told the story of a young man I met who went to Japan in the late Sixties to study Rinzai Zen but left after two weeks because the practice was too rigorous and he just couldn't do it. Several years later he returned to try it again. After three days he was in such pain that he was about to give up, and then the thought came to him, "I'll die before I leave." With this resolve the koan that he was working on broke open and he went up to his teacher and presented his insight. His teacher approved and the young man later became a Zen teacher himself.

I told the group that even if you are not practicing Rinzai Zen or in the heat of a difficult retreat, this is still the kind of determination that is required. In your daily practice and in your daily life, when there is the urge to drift of into daydreaming rather than staying right here in the present moment, say to yourself, "I'll die before leaving right here."

On the way home Ellen was struck by the way I applied this idea to our everyday practice and life. She thought it was a good way to encourage people to bring some energy, determination, and intensity to their practice. We reflected how this idea might also apply to a long-term relationship: until you decide you are not leaving, and are willing to drop your self-centered views, the energy and determination is not there to work hard enough to make the relationship really come to life.

Last summer I (Ellen) gave a Zen workshop at a nursing conference in Boulder, Colorado. Charles came along to hear what I had to say and to participate in the workshop. Afterward, one of the participants came up to Charles and told him that she got just what she needed most at this time in her life from attending the workshop. She went on to say that what moved her most was watching the way Charles listened to me—his attentiveness and the expression on his face.

HUMAN BEINGS AND OUR RELATIONSHIPS are infinitely complex and subtle, so there is no end to the ways you can learn about yourself and your partner. If you commit to being a lifelong learner, what can you learn about love? What can your relationship be? In the freshness and newness of each moment you can learn the heart's secret of falling in love over and over again.

In our twenties we were in love and felt like we had our whole lives ahead of us. Now that we are in our fifties, we have a greater sense of how precious life is. In the past several years several of our close friends have experienced the death of a husband or wife. This struck close to home and woke us up to the need not to leave things unsaid, to say, "I love you"—and to be sure to *show* each other how much the other is loved. Our life together does not lie ahead of us. It takes place right now.

ON THE CUTTING EDGE

ONE EVENING while playing a game of hearts, Roshi Kennedy told us that years ago when he was living in Japan, Koun Yamada Roshi invited him over for tea after *sesshin*. Mrs. Yamada was there and as they were talking around the table Yamada Roshi got up and served the tea. Roshi Kennedy told us, "This is not your usual Japanese husband." This is not your usual Zen master either!

Both Yamada Roshi, a lay teacher rather than a professional priest, and his wife had full-time careers outside the home. Yamada Roshi rode the train each day to Tokyo to work as president of the Tokyo Kembikyoin Medical Center, and in the evening and on weekends he taught Zen to students from Japan, America, and around the world. For us he is a beacon lighting the way and showing that it is possible to be both happily married and utterly committed to Zen. Throughout history, in both the Buddhist and Christian worlds, in order to pursue a contemplative path and devote oneself to spiritual development, it was considered necessary to live a monastic life. This followed the example of Jesus, who did not marry, or Buddha, who left his wife and child behind to seek enlightenment. Perhaps this was necessary in the past, given cultural context and practical constraints (though one never knows!) but now our culture has changed. We have more leisure time than ever before. The householder role is no longer inextricably linked with the responsibility for feeding and raising a large family. We have more options and flexibility. What was viewed as necessary or inevitable in the past may be just one of many possible lifestyles for serious spiritual seekers of today. One Zen teacher we know, Barbara Craig, is a Sister of Mercy. She has been a nun for over 50 years. One day as we were walking along the Jersey Shore together, she told us that there are not many young people joining her order these days, and so the community is becoming smaller. However, she said that their "associates" are growing in number. Associates are laypeople who affiliate with the sisters to support their vision and join in their work.

In this country, most of the people interested in various Buddhist meditation paths have a partner or family. It is time to clearly acknowledge couple or family spirituality as a valid path, not lesser in any way than the path of the monastic. Each path has its own beauty, its own song to sing and work to do.

Some people practicing Zen in a monastic setting have encountered problems with the amount of time they are away from partners and children. Although a serious spiritual practice does demand a commitment of time, energy, and resources, it does not require extensive time living in a monastery. We need to expand our ideas about the settings where practice can take place. Practice does not take place just on the cushion or at retreat. We can be aware of self-centered feelings arising in the context of daily life with a partner and choose not to add to them with our thoughts and habitual reactions. In the workplace and at home we can work with the same attention we bring to work period in a monastery. Every moment of daily life is an opportunity to choose to be present or lost in a dream. The monastic model is not the only path to spiritual development.

In the Native American traditions the medicine men and women are usually married. Experiencing firsthand the ways of a husband or wife and parent helps them to know and credibly serve the needs of their people. It helps them to grow in life and wisdom.

In the late '60s and early '70s we had the privilege of knowing a very wise Hopi Elder named David Monongye. In the years since, we have come across several pictures of him in books. In one he is face to face with the Dalai Lama. In another, he is part of a Native Peoples delegation to a conference in Geneva, Switzerland. David lived on the Hopi reservation in Hotevilla, and often after the dances or ceremonies held in the village he invited us into his red sandstone home to tell stories and talk for a while. There were dirt floors, no electricity, and his wife, Nora, cooked on a wood stove. She offered us blue piki bread and coffee.

They lived simply as a couple with integrity following the Hopi way. Every activity of daily life, the way David grew the corn and the way Nora made bread, were part of their spiritual world. They were a source of inspiration to Hopis and others to remain in touch with the spiritual in everyday life. Knowing them was a formative experience for us in our view of married spirituality. We could see, taste, and feel that married life and deep spirituality can go hand in hand.

In the famous and well-loved poems of Cold Mountain, the poet tells of his peaceful life in the mountains with the clacking sound of his wife working at her loom, the jabbering of his son at play, and the singing of birds. He asks, "Who comes to commend me on my way of life?" and he answers, "Well, a woodcutter sometimes passes by."

The path of a couple or family engaged in a meditation practice and devoted to spiritual insight is self-affirming. Even if only one partner meditates and is actively engaged in spiritual practice, it can enrich the relationship if the partners respect the differences in their spiritual paths and are committed to the spiritual well-being of one another. It is possible to be both deeply human, fully experiencing ordinary life, and at the same time deeply spiritual, awakening to your essential nature and expressing this insight in compassionate action in the home and in the world.

Although it is clearly possible, we are on the cutting edge of making this possibility a reality. How do you retain the discipline and rigor of spiritual practice in the midst of an active life in the world? Anyone who has spent time in a monastery knows that it is not all meditation and chanting. Many hours a day are spent weeding the garden, cooking meals, doing office work, and cleaning bathrooms. If you apply the same attention and vigor to your job and chores at home, you find you can accomplish a great deal and still have time to meditate daily. If you plan your life carefully, you can make time to attend meditation retreats on a regular basis.

We need to empower one another to create a new model for relationship that promotes spiritual development—a new framework for spirituality in relationship. There is no need to sacrifice life itself for wisdom. The two are inseparable. There is no need to neglect your relationship in order to develop spiritually. Doing this misses the point. Spiritual practice is about realizing how precious your life, *all* of it, really is. Special moments and occasions with partners and children cannot be recaptured. Attending to your partner and working on your relationship are parts of your spiritual practice and enhance your spiritual development. It is possible to lead, and indeed necessary to lead, a balanced life.

Monastics, couples, and those who are single, whether by choice or by circumstance, can work together transcending these categories to develop the spiritual potential of whoever is interested in this work. While volumes have been written about monastic spirituality, little attention has been given to spiritual development in relationship. We need to discover and describe how relationships and spiritual practice can be mutually enhancing.

One of the most famous of koans is "the sound of one hand clapping." We invite you to listen to this sound the next time you see a couple united in wisdom and love walking hand in hand.

THIS MOMENT TOGETHER

THERE IS A ZEN STORY about a hermit who lived all alone in a little hut up in the mountains. One day while the hermit was out gathering berries, thieves came and stole the few possessions he had. They took everything and then they burned the hut to the ground. That evening when the hermit arrived home to find everything gone, he walked over to where his hut had been and sat contentedly down in ashes, surrounded only by moonlight. What is this moonlight? What is it that cannot be taken away or consumed by flames? What is it that keeps us going even when the going gets rough?

We hear so much these days about living in the present moment. Don't worry about the past or the future because the present moment is all you have. You may get a serious illness or get in an automobile accident and die at any time. Reflecting in this way, you realize that you better appreciate your life and your loved ones while you can. Life is precious, and you don't want it to just pass you by. You need to say and do the things that are meaningful and important to you right now. Begin living fully and appreciating each moment as it comes.

It's valuable to gain even partial insight into this and to try to live it out—but many people stop here. They think that if they appreciate the beauty of a sunrise, speak in a loving way to their family members, or enjoy a great meal that is being in the present moment. These are good experiences and actions, and a step in the right direction, but the present moment is not just the present moment.

There is a Zen saying, "First there is a mountain, then there is no mountain, then there is." At first you experience the beauty and magnificence of the mountain. This is the level with which we are all familiar. You take a hike in the mountains and enjoy smelling the fresh air, the company of your partner, and the colors and textures of the plants and trees all around you. This is what is called the realm of form. From a Zen perspective it is real. It is here to be appreciated, enjoyed, and cared for, but it is not all that there is.

Through meditation practice, you can directly experience the essential nature of the mountain, which is one with your own essential nature, or the essential nature of your partner, the trees, and everything else. This is the experience of "no mountain." There is no thing. Nothing is separate. You directly experience oneness. This is the realm of the formless. The experience of oneness is deeply satisfying. It is what you long for deep down. You see that everything is moonlight—but still we don't stop here. We return to daily life, allowing the experience of oneness to illuminate and shine through all that we see and do. Now there is a mountain again and it is magical. It sparkles and teems with life. This is what is called "just this."

This is what living in the present moment really means. You experience that your partner is the moonlight. It is this experience that keeps love alive, moment by moment for as long as you open to its radiance. This moment can be magical.

One thing that is true about a magic moment is that you cannot hold on to it. You can only live and appreciate it fully while it is here and then move on to be fully present again in a new moment, a new day. Staying fresh and new for each other keeps a relationship alive and vital. You don't dwell on the past, although you cherish your memories of special times and of lessons learned. You don't live in the future, although you share hopes and dreams for your future together. You change and grow together, moment by moment, creating new magic in your life right now.

Sometimes in a relationship a magic moment is crystal clear like a moonlit, starry night without a cloud in the sky to obstruct your view. It is smooth sailing hand in hand out across the sky. At other times, things are more muddled and confused. Emotions are mixed and like hazy moonlight on a foggy night. Nevertheless, even here there is a magical quality as you journey onward together not knowing where you will land next.

There is a koan in the *Blue Cliff Record* about sixteen bodhisattvas who went down for their bath one morning, as they always did at the same time each day. But this time, as the warm water touched them, they had a great insight. Later in describing their experience one bodhisattva said, "We experienced the subtle and clear touch, have attained buddhahood, and still retain it."

We must not skip over the fact that the bodhisattvas exclaim that the insight is clear *and subtle*. If you try to hold on to it, it becomes just a memory. In order to retain it, you must keep going, seeing into its infinite subtlety, and expressing it in your life.

At the end of a recent weeklong sesshin at St. Benedict's

Monastery in Snowmass, Colorado, Bill and Stevie, a couple we have been meditating with for many years, celebrated their thirty-seventh anniversary. They brought bottles of champagne to share with everyone at our concluding lunch. They said the occasion was particularly significant for them since they spent their honeymoon in nearby Glenwood Springs. And now they had returned many years later to the same mountains to spend a week meditating together. The mountains were the same, but Bill and Stevie had grown and changed in so many ways, and their love was now deeper and more mature, yet still fresh and new.

In order for a relationship to stay fresh and grow, you need to continuously explore and discover its infinite subtlety. Luckily, this takes a lifetime—and if you practice this kind of openness you will be surprised by something new moment by moment and year after year.

ZEN INSIGHTS THAT TRANSFORM RELATIONSHIPS

KNOWING YOURSELF AND NO-SELF

K NOWING YOURSELF is a prerequisite for a fulfilling long-term relationship. Each brings him- or herself as a gift to the other, and each receives the other as gift. But first you need to be able to stand on your own two feet without excessive leaning or clinging that wears the other down. You need some degree of emotional and spiritual maturity in order to enter into a relationship of mutual giving and receiving. Of course many of us do not have a well-developed sense of self, and this contributes greatly to relationship problems. Luckily, if we are open and diligent, we can learn as we go along with the relationship itself as a teacher and with a spiritual practice that encourages the ongoing psychological as well as spiritual development of the individual. Having a well-developed sense of self is a key aspect of being psychologically healthy and balanced. You have developed your abilities and are able to work to support yourself. You know who you are, what you like, and what you want in life. You are in touch with your values and spirituality. You are not overly egotistical and self-centered and have concern for the needs and feelings of others. What we are speaking of here is all pretty basic psychology, but many people think that because it is obvious, they can skip this step. Skipping this step usually leads to rough traveling somewhere down the road in relationships and on the spiritual journey.

That is why it is often helpful for many people to get some psychological counseling or therapy before, during, or after a relationship to learn more about themselves. The same is true on the spiritual path. No matter how long you have been on the road, you can always benefit from learning more about yourself. Psychological development enhances both relationships and spiritual development.

A while ago our paths crossed with an old friend we had not seen in many years. He was now happily married, and he invited us out to dinner to meet his wife. We all had a great evening laughing and talking. He and his wife were so visibly in love with one another. He said that, although his decades of full-time spiritual practice were very fulfilling, he never had a relationship that worked out well at all. So, when a friend suggested that he go for therapy, he decided to give it a try. He couldn't say enough about how much it helped him. Shortly thereafter he met his wife, and they have been very happily married for several years now.

Relationships are most successful when psychological and spiritual development take place hand in hand.

One of the benefits of meditation is that when you sit down in silence on a regular basis you get to know yourself better. In zazen you sit up straight and alert on a three-foot-by-three-foot mat without moving, and in that silence and stillness you notice things you never noticed before. You notice how busy your mind is—full of thoughts, stories, worries, judgments, and plans. With continued daily practice, the mental chatter settles down and you begin to notice patterns in the thoughts that persist, coming up over and over again. They reveal to you something about yourself. In the process, you learn about the nature of the mind itself.

In meditation you learn about your emotions and feel them arise in your body. You see how the flame of emotion is fueled and fanned by your thoughts and by the stories you tell yourself about an event. It gradually dies down and loses its grip on your attention. Soon you are on to something else. Learning about your feelings and the way they rise and fall is one of the things you learn in meditation that is most directly applicable to relationships. A clear knowledge of this, both mentally and in your body, enables you to become less emotionally reactive and less likely to get hurt or fly off the handle in your interactions with your partner.

One of the things the two of us have become more aware of from our meditation practice is our tendency to worry about little things when there are no major crises present in our lives at the time, as if to fulfill some kind of "worry quota." When a major crisis occurs such as a medical emergency or death in the family, the little worries and irritations are dropped as our attention and energy are directed toward coping with the crisis. Grumbling over small hassles and inconveniences needlessly adds tension and drains energy from the relationship. Sitting in meditation, noticing our habitual tendency to worry, we become aware of anxiety arising in the body and mind and can choose to not add to it. We are quick to see our habit of worrying and notice the sensation of anxiety just as it arises. Rather than amplifying it with thoughts, stories, and interpretations, we allow it to naturally die down again.

This awareness carries over into daily life. Recently we went out of town and left our car in long-term parking at the airport. When we returned home we found someone had run into it, knocking it into a diagonal position in the parking space and denting in the right rear side. Although a situation like this is upsetting, we found we were able to take it in stride. It was late at night and we were tired, but we did not take our frustration out on one another. We simply got a security officer to fill out an incident report and the next day called the insurance company to find out about getting the car repaired.

It is so easy for us both to get angry, worried, and upset about something like this—and it can even mar our enjoyment of a trip. If we are inattentive, this stress can carry over into the next week, adding stress to the relationship as we work through getting it fixed. In this kind of situation, it helps us to recognize our feelings as they arise and, without repressing or denying them, simply be aware of them and feel them, without acting on them by grumbling or taking it out on our partner. This is spiritual practice in daily life in relationship.

While sitting in meditation, you also get to know yourself physically. In stillness you become familiar with every bone and muscle in your body—a pain in your knee, an ache in your shoulder, an itch on your nose. It demands physical discipline and endurance to sit up straight without moving, but it doesn't just result in discomfort there are pleasant sensations too—the slow gentle rising and falling of your belly, the spacious feeling of a tall balanced spine, a cool breeze across your cheek. You feel sensations you might otherwise miss. You get to know your body. When you are awake and aware in meditation you are awake and aware not just mentally but with every cell in your body. This allows you to bring more of yourself into your relationship and to be fully present in body, mind, and spirit with your partner. So in order to improve your relationships and nurture your spiritual development it is necessary to get to know yourself better, but this alone is not enough. You also need to be able to see beyond the limited ego or separate self. This requires deep spiritual practice because it cannot be grasped intellectually. It must be directly experienced with your whole being.

A good koan on this theme of knowing yourself concerns a monk named Guizong, who went to Zen Master Fayan and said, "My name is Guizong, I ask you, what is Buddha?" Fayan said, "You are Guizong." Fayan wants Guizong to experience that Buddha is not outside himself. His own essential nature is the same as the essential nature of Buddha, and he is one with everything else in the universe. In this experience, you directly realize oneness, that you are not separate. This is sometimes called "no self" because you see that, from this perspective, there is no separate self. You are Buddha. You are the good earth, the trees, the mountain lion, the moon, and the farthest star. You are your lover there beside you.

The experience of oneness, or nonseparation, is joyful, powerful, and liberating. It energizes and inspires you to engage in compassionate action. The direct experience of "no self" allows you to see that you are larger than you think, larger than your small limited ego or self. With expanded vision, you are able to behave in a kinder and more loving way. This can have a profound and positive influence on your relationships. When you do something kind for your partner such as prepare a special meal, give a back rub, or run an errand during a busy time, it is not done with an attitude or feeling that you are being *magnanimous* in doing something for another. It is done out of a deep sense of connection and oneness. The experience of oneness, or no-self illuminates, and expands your appreciation for yourself as a unique individual. You don't need to look somewhere else or to someone else. Take a good look for yourself. See yourself, for yourself. You are not Buddha. Don't try to be Buddha. Be the best *you* you can be, with all your frailties, sensitivities, and strengths.

This brings you full circle. You begin with knowing and developing yourself. Then you work on opening to and directly experiencing that which is beyond or larger than yourself. In this experience you see that it is nothing other than yourself. It is just this, just this life, so live it fully with awareness, appreciation, and gratitude.

In terms of relationship, bring your best self, who you really are, into the relationship. Be yourself. Admit your mistakes and know your limitations. Stay in touch with who you are deep down and with your own unique gifts. Develop and share your talents and freely express your own unique experience of life.

Once at a Zen retreat Ellen gave a *teisho* on this koan about Guizong and Fayan. Afterward when Roshi Kennedy got up to speak, he said, "I wish someone had told me that, a long time ago when I was a young man, 'You are Bob.' It would have saved me a lot of trouble." Then he paused and said, "Of course, they did, but I couldn't hear it."

BOUNDARIES AND NO BOUNDARIES

WHENEVER WE GIVE Zen retreats and talks, no matter where we go, there are always several therapists in the group. When we start to speak about "no boundaries" you can see the therapists begin to shift in their seats and a look of discomfort come over their faces. Boundaries are a very important issue in the field of psychology, and many books and articles have been written on the topic. Boundaries differentiate between the roles of the therapist and client and clarify appropriate behaviors for each in the therapeutic relationship. When boundaries are violated it can cause great harm to the client. So as Zen teachers speaking of "no boundaries" let us first affirm the value of boundaries not only in psychotherapy but in our everyday relationships as well.

Boundaries define who you are as an individual. They help you know where you end and the other person begins. This allows you to make decisions in your life consistent with your own values, feelings, needs, and opinions and not be unduly influenced by others. Boundaries help you set limits so others don't take advantage of you. They separate your responsibilities and duties from the responsibilities and duties of others. This divides duties into manageable parts so you don't become overwhelmed, feeling responsible for everything.

You don't get exhausted trying to do everything yourself. Successful relationships depend on each person doing his or her part.

In the early '80s Charles traveled to New York City for a month to study Zen with Bernie Glassman, and while there, he worked in the bakery that provided a livelihood for the Zen Community of New York. When he came home he said he thought it might be a good idea for us to move there. At the time we had a four-year-old daughter and a home in the country. I (Ellen) told him that I didn't mind moving in order to study Zen, but living in a big city like New York was beyond my limits. I let him know that he was free to go there as much as he wanted, but that I was a country girl at heart and, for my own mental health, needed to live in a simpler, more natural place with a slower pace.

In this instance, I was able to know my limits and maintain boundaries I could live with. It was a decision that worked out well for us both in the long run.

There is a Zen expression, "snow in the silver bowl." It emphasizes the importance of differences, or boundaries. Even though it is hard to distinguish between pure white snow and its reflection in a shiny silver bowl, we can distinguish the snow from the bowl. It is like water in a clear glass. We can tell the difference between the water and the glass. We can make out the form of a snow-white bird standing on the snowy hillside. Differences are important. Although in our essential nature we are united, in the relative, there are boundaries, and they allow us to be recognized as separate entities. This beautiful Zen imagery encourages us to appreciate both oneness and differences, the Absolute and the relative. It is not an either/or situation.

In the relative, boundaries are essential. One of the most exquisite boundaries of all is our skin. It is a flexible, semipermeable membrane that protects us from the loss of precious bodily fluids and from the invasion of infectious microorganisms. It is sensitive to the pain of a hot flame that warns us to recoil and to the soothing touch of a lover that draws us closer. Many people think that they end with their skin, but that is not the whole picture.

Zen meditation is one path that can help us see more of the whole picture. Zen is an approach to meditation and life that leads to the direct experience of nonseparation, or vast, unbounded clarity. Zen has its roots in Buddhism that includes teachings on *shunyata*, or emptiness. Sometimes when people hear the term *emptiness* they think it means some kind of a void. Others think it sounds like an experience of depersonalization, annihilation, or lack of identity. However, what emptiness is referring to is an experience of no boundaries. It is empty of boundaries and divisions. Without boundaries, there is no separation—no dualistic division between body and mind, inside and outside, subject and object, self and other.

It is an experience that transcends thought and intellect, and that's why the practice of meditation is necessary. In fact, it is thoughts and concepts that divide. When we think of a concept such as dog, in the mind we separate out the animals from the plants, and then the dogs from the cats, horses, and birds. Thoughts and concepts are a way to divide into categories and organize phenomena. This is very useful in order to function in the world. When we meditate, of course, we do not lose our ability to reason and think. What we do is take a break from our usual way of thinking so that, in silence, we can open to other ways of knowing and being.

In silence, you open to the perception that, in addition to boundaries and separation or individuation, there is nonseparation, oneness, and the experience of no boundaries. This experience is unifying and adds a rich, new dimension to relationships. You experience that unity does not result in annihilation or being engulfed. It is an experience that is expansive, freeing, and empowering. You are now free and flexible enough to experience and appreciate both boundaries and no boundaries simultaneously.

The most widely used book of koans is *The Gateless Gate*. This name highlights the ability of the Zen approach to allow you to embrace perspectives that seem to be opposites. The purpose of a gate is to keep something in or to keep something out—and so what is a gateway without a gate? When we lived out on the Navajo reservation, it was open range. There were no gates and there were no fences either. As you drove down the highway you had to be on the lookout for cattle or sheep in the road. The livestock were free to roam. The phrase *gateless gate* points to the fact that there are no boundaries, gates, or fences in your mind other than those you have erected yourself. Zen practice can help you see and move through these self-imposed barriers so you are free to roam the whole universe, unobstructed.

Often we erect walls within ourselves to protect us from the pain of separation and rejection. In self-defense, we reinforce the very walls that keep us separate from the connection, acceptance, and love that we long for. In the safety and silence of meditation we can see and experience this on a deep emotional and physical level. With time and deepening insight, we gain the strength, trust, and confidence to let down the walls.

There is a Zen verse that says:

> *House demolished, the person perished, neither inside nor outside,*
> *Where can body and mind hide their forms?*

Without walls and boundaries, we experience that we are not separate in body or mind. There is no separate self that needs protection. There is nobody home. There is no one inside the house in need of protection from those on the outside. When the walls come down, you are one with everything and everyone and with the whole universe. The experience of oneness or unity is naturally expressed in love. Your relationships are now rooted in an experience of unbounded love.

The experience of no boundaries carries you beyond the boundaries of space and time. The particular love in your life, right here and now, is the experience of eternal love.

The experience of boundaries and the experience of no boundaries each bring their wisdom to enrich relationships. Boundaries help you remain focused. One couple I know is employed at the same hospital. One day I overheard the supervisor ask the husband if he could work an extra shift over the weekend. He replied in a lighthearted tone, "I'll have to check with my primary boss." He was referring to his wife and his response demonstrated his awareness of the need to maintain boundaries that protect and preserve their time together as a couple. Boundaries are needed to maintain balance and give a couple time and privacy, free from children, relatives, friends, and too many outside activities.

At the same time, experience of no boundaries frees us to let down our barriers and truly love. We can heed the advice of Robert Frost, who encourages us to go beyond the saying that has been handed down to us, "Good fences make good neighbors." Before reinforcing walls and boundaries we should take a good look at what it is we are walling in or walling out. There are places where no walls are needed, and when you open to these places you open to limitless possibilities, beyond the boundaries of your furthest imagination.

Oneness is already here. It is not something that needs to be attained. Awakening to oneness or the experience of "no boundaries" is an ongoing process available to all of us in every moment. We need to sit down in the deep silence of meditation and see the walls we have built around ourselves and with this awareness stop reinforcing them. Our human tendency to wall ourselves off and protect our territory is so ingrained that even the most enlightened among us continue to sit each day to see this ever more clearly.

Even seeking out a path of spiritual practice shows you have some sense of something greater than your present experience of yourself and your life. From the beginning of your practice, if meditation didn't bring you some sense of peace and connection, you probably wouldn't return to meditate again. These initial inklings of oneness increase gradually and sometimes in sudden leaps as you continue to meditate each day. All along the way, what is important is your intention and attention to bringing this growing sense of oneness, openness, and connection into your daily life and relationship with your partner.

NOT ONE—NOT TWO

RECENTLY we attended the wedding of a young woman we knew during the years she was growing up in our neighborhood. At her wedding there was a special table up in the front of the church, and in the middle of it was a white pillar candle with a white taper candle to each side of it. As part of the ceremony, the parents of the bride and groom each lit one of the tapers and gave it to their adult child. The bride and groom then joined the flames of their two candles and together lit the pillar candle. Then they returned the lighted tapers to their original places, still burning brightly.

This is a beautiful ritual to symbolize that when we unite with another in marriage something new is created. We are one couple, one family. At the same time, each person remains an individual. Simultaneously both of these realities are honored and nurtured. The light of all three candles is the same light.

In Zen we say, "Not one, not two." "Not one" means that we cannot ignore differences among individuals. Each of us is unique and that is what gives life its texture and richness. "Not two" acknowledges the unity of everything in its essential nature. The experience of unity expands our awareness and capacity for love.

There is a deep human longing to relate well with a partner, friends, family members, and people at work. When meaningful relationships are formed, it is one of the most important and satisfying aspects of a person's life. Relationships are also the source of some of life's greatest pain and disappointment. Volumes have been written on how to improve relationships, and much of this advice is useful. Yet somehow relationship problems still plague us and remain a major cause of human suffering.

In the everyday or relative world, which is the perspective of most people, relationships occur between self and other. The world of self and other is the realm of duality. Even marriage and family therapists, who use a systems psychology approach and take into consideration the influence of each person on the family system, are still dealing with parts of a system and the interactions and multiple influences of the parts. This is a step forward in understanding the complexity of relationships, but it is not enough. It still views people as separate selves—albeit ones interacting with one another—and remains thus dualistic, and ultimately limited. What is needed is a giant leap forward to the direct experience of non-separation, or oneness.

The experience of essential nature, or oneness, is available to each of us right here and now. What obscures oneness from your view is thinking and conditioning. You have been raised to view yourself as a separate self, with everything from the skin outward being seen as other. While this viewpoint has survival value in the relative world and cannot be ignored, it is, at the same time, a limiting perspective that creates much misery.

But again it's important to stress that experiencing oneness does not negate the relative perspective of "twoness," the difference between self and other. Rather, it vastly expands your vision—so much so that it gives you a completely new perspective. When we fall in love or make love, the ego boundaries come down to some extent and it is a very positive experience, but it is limited. When the walls come down completely, the experience of oneness is of cosmic proportion. It transforms your life. The experience of oneness is so expansive and fulfilling that many people who open to it, either spontaneously or through meditation practice, stop there. They view everything in terms of oneness. Statements that are true from an Absolute perspective are now mistakenly applied to situations in the relative world of cause and effect—and you hear of many "enlightened" people with relationship disasters.

The problem here is ignoring the relative. There is the need to take a further step in learning how to actualize your realization of the Absolute, or world of oneness, in everyday life in the relative world. The Heart Sutra says, "Form is precisely emptiness, emptiness is precisely form." Form refers to the world of things, the relative. Emptiness refers to the world of no-thing, the world of oneness, the Absolute. There is no Absolute apart from the relative. It is through the relative that the Absolute is known. That is why relationships are so important. Roshi Kennedy often says, "You can't put your arms around the Absolute." The Absolute is manifested in a particular person and a particular relationship. Nonduality is directly experienced in "just this" relationship with your particular partner.

In an enlightened relationship, both oneness and differences are perceived and lived out simultaneously. But it is not enough to understand this intellectually. Nonduality must be experienced directly and actualized in the relative world on an ongoing basis. Enlightenment is not something that is attained once and for all. It is a moment-by-moment process of being open to the expanded vision of nonduality. In the same way, enlightened relationships are not attained once and for all. They also require moment-by-moment opening to both oneness and differences. The direct experience of oneness, or nonseparation, is so enlivening, soothing, and boundless that it allows you to experience differences, individuality, and separation without feeling threatened, abandoned, or deprived. Paradoxically, the experience of Absolute oneness enhances your appreciation of the relative world of differences.

Often at retreats when people see us both sitting in meditation side by side on our mats, they comment, "It must be great to have someone to share this with, someone on the same spiritual path." Of course it is wonderful to have a life partner who shares a deep interest in spirituality and mediation—someone to go with to retreats, someone to talk with about spiritual matters and insights.

But even so it is important to realize that, although we share much spiritually and are united in our spiritual practice, each of us travels his or her own unique spiritual path. Although from the outside, sitting side by side in the same posture, we look like we are doing the same thing, the experience of meditation is different for each of us at any particular moment in time. We each walk along the path of Zen at different rates and with different lessons that need to be learned and unlearned.

We each have our own spiritual path whether it looks the same or different. It is like the old spiritual, "Lonesome Valley," which tells us, "Nobody else can walk it for us. We have to walk that valley for ourselves." No matter how much we may love our partner, we cannot take away our partner's pain, we cannot "make" our partner happy, and we cannot "enlighten" our partner. Each person must walk the spiritual path for her- or himself. So even if we travel together, we travel alone.

Recognizing this aloneness is essential for togetherness.

ALL THINGS CHANGE

WE CANNOT HELP but notice that everything around us is constantly changing. Today it is cold and rainy; yesterday it was sunny and clear. The leaves that were once overhead on the branches of trees are now beneath our feet breaking down into topsoil.

We can also see this in our homes. You discover that the walls need painting periodically, the light bulbs need replacing, and the appliances get old and give out one by one so you have to go buy new ones. As good as it may look now, the place is never cleaned up once and for all.

In meditation you experience that it isn't just the outside world that is constantly changing. You find your inner world is also in a constant state of flux. Thoughts, emotions, and sensations arise, one after the other, changing from moment to moment. Sometimes you feel calm and peaceful and at other times restless or worried. You become familiar with internal change. With this familiarity comes an increased ability to not get stuck, but rather move along with the flow of change. When you fall in love, life is good. You feel happy, excited, and full of life. All of your senses are more open, colors are brighter, and music is sweeter. You feel you have found what you have been looking for all your life. You hope this wonderful feeling will last forever. But just as the seasons change and you cannot keep the snow from falling, relationships change. Just as a house changes and needs constant attention, so does a relationship. As you learn to accept continuous change within yourself, you come to accept changes that occur in relationships.

We are happy to acknowledge constant change as a basic fact of life when we are in a difficult situation. One couple we know was having great difficulty adjusting to the husband having to work evening shift. The wife worked day shift. They were really frustrated with only seeing each other on Saturday and Sunday. Eventually they decided that they could no longer put up with it, and the husband started looking for another job. A few days into his search, his seniority number came up at his current job and he finally got to move to day shift. It was a happy change.

When you don't like your current circumstances, it is easy to embrace and hope for change. On the other hand, when your life is going great, you try to hold on to what you have and don't want things to change. When you finally find the perfect lover, you don't want him or her to change and you don't like to think of the time when he or she will die. But change and impermanence are a fact of life in this world. When you cling and try to control in an effort to hold change at bay, you cause yourself even greater suffering. While you are busy putting all your energy into clinging and controlling, you miss experiencing your lover as he or she is right now. You miss your precious life as it passes by unnoticed.

There is a Zen story about change. Once a monk by the name of Damei went to Zen Master Mazu and asked him, "What is Buddha?" Mazu replied, "The very mind is Buddha." Hearing this,

Damei was awakened. He clearly saw that everything was one with his essential nature, with his very mind, with the essential nature of Buddha. With this opening, he decided to go off to the forest to meditate and mature his insight. Nobody knew where he went or heard from him for many years.

One day a young monk was making a pilgrimage and stopped to ask directions from a woodcutter living deep in the woods. The woodcutter told him, "Go on following the flow of water." This was good advice on a practical level since following the flow of the river keeps you from walking around and around in circles when you are lost in the thick forest and can't see where you are going. But the monk knew that the response also had a deeper meaning. He sensed that this man was a sage telling him that it is best to go with the flow of changing circumstances in your life. Don't try to swim upstream or try to hold back the river. Be open to life as it presents itself.

Later on in his journey, the young monk ended up at the monastery of Zen Master Mazu and told him about his encounter with the woodcutter. Hearing the story, Mazu thought this wood-cutter might be Damei who went off to the woods many years before. He sent the young monk to visit the woodcutter again to find out if he was Damei. The young monk went back to see the wood-cutter and asked, "What is Buddha?" The woodcutter replied, "The very mind is Buddha." Hearing this the monk told him that now when asked, "What is Buddha?" Mazu says, "No mind, no Buddha."

Hearing this, Damei tells the monk, "'No mind, no Buddha' is fine for Mazu but for me it is still 'The very mind is Buddha.'" When the young monk reported to Mazu what Damei had said, Mazu exclaimed, "The plum has ripened!" (The name Damei means "big plum.") Damei calls it as he sees it, and Mazu acknowledges the spiritual maturity of Damei in presenting the unique flavor and emphasis of his own experience regardless of what Mazu is into these days.

Mazu changed the emphasis of his teaching because when people heard his earlier teaching, many got stuck there intellectualizing. They made mind and Buddha into concepts, into things. They became trapped in form, so he needed to change the angle or emphasis of his teaching in order to free them.

But Damei was already free. He continued to honor and celebrate the insight that awakened and freed him. It was not that Mazu's first teaching was untrue or that it was outdated. Mazu changed his response according to his circumstances and experience. Damei stayed with his original experience. You do not need to change just for the sake of change nor do you need to feel compelled to jump on the latest bandwagon.

There are many lessons for couples in this story. It shows us that frequently, due to varying circumstances, we change. Sometimes one person in a relationship changes in a way that the other does not, and even if you do change in similar ways you won't always change at the same rate. Changing at different rates doesn't necessarily mean that one person is more advanced or that the other is left behind. Nor does changing in a way that heightens differences between you and your partner mean you are wrong, disloyal, or growing apart. And, on the other side, *not* changing doesn't mean you have failed to develop or you are too old-fashioned. Amid the changes, each person must be true to his or her experience of life. Even if you are different in more ways than you once were, you can continue to appreciate each other and to hold one another in high regard. Increased differences do not need to lead to increased distance between partners. If change and differences are embraced and respected rather than resisted they can result in increased texture and richness in the relationship.

For a relationship to grow and thrive, each person needs to feel free to change. Each has the right to change his or her mind. What you say today is today's answer. When you say something different tomorrow, you are speaking in different circumstances, from a new viewpoint. As Walt Whitman wrote, "Do I contradict myself? Very well then I contradict myself (I am large, I contain multitudes.)" You need to be able to trust your partner to share with you who he or she is today. This immediacy is true intimacy. You don't want to relate to a mask, an empty shell, or an image of who your partner was yesterday. Each needs to reveal who he or she is in this moment.

Change is often unpredictable. You cannot predict how you will change. Nor can you predict how your partner will change. But what remains steadfast and gives you hope is confidence in each partner's ability and effort to change, learn, and grow. You also need confidence that each partner holds, in his or her heart and intentions, the well-being and spiritual fulfillment of the other. Rooted in this intention, change, although challenging at times, is experienced as freshness, the cutting edge, and the unfolding of potential. Exciting new potential for each individual and for the

relationship is realized as you change and grow. Change is a vital
force that keeps your relationship fresh, exciting, and alive.

EQUALITY AND BALANCE

O<small>N MANY OCCASIONS</small> as a child, I (Ellen) remember having a candy bar to split with a friend. One of us would unwrap the candy bar and carefully cut it exactly in half. Then as an extra measure of friendship and good faith, the one who cut it would let the other choose first whichever half she wanted, just in case there was any perceived inequity of portions. This ritual worked for us as children, and the spirit of share and share alike was highly valued. We remained friends, and each satisfied her need for fairness, justice, and equity—but there are many things in life that cannot be divided and shared so neatly.

Equality in a relationship does not mean that each person gets exactly the same amount of each resource available to the couple. What it means is that the well-being and spiritual development of each partner is equally considered and supported. One couple we know decided that the husband, Jason, would continue working while the wife, Emily, took several years off from her job to develop her talent as a dancer. Jason enjoyed attending Emily's performances and was proud of her accomplishments, and Julie's pursuing of her dream brought fresh energy into the relationship. This becomes a challenging balancing act since you need to take into account the well-being of each partner as well as the well-being of the relationship. Going back to the three wedding candles described in an earlier chapter, there are three flames to keep burning, warm and bright. This takes goodwill, hard work, and wisdom.

It is only in very recent times that equality for women has even been considered in marriage or in spiritual endeavors. We are pioneers. Equality in relationships is still in an experimental stage. It helps to keep this in mind as we struggle to work out the quirks and snags as they pop up along the way. Even couples with the best relationships grapple with how two people can develop their talents and careers in a satisfying way while also having a meaningful life together. When you add to the mix a child or two, it becomes much more complicated and, for many, more rewarding as well.

In the spiritual arena, we are also in the early days of equality for women. Many religious organizations in this country and around the world still bar women from being ordained or from holding a leadership position. For centuries the spiritual insights of women have not been acknowledged or valued. This remains a fresh wound in need of sensitivity and healing. At the same time, there is an air of excitement and energy as we now have an unprecedented opportunity to create organizations and venues where women's spirituality is nurtured and fully recognized.

Equality can take many different forms. In many relationships both the husband and wife work outside the home—sometimes by choice and sometimes by necessity. Yet amid the demands of work and home, each partner needs time for spiritual development. Quiet time alone restores balance to a busy life and gives you the opportunity for developing your spirituality. This can take many different forms.

As a couple, we both share an interest in Zen, and have each cho-sen to take on a leadership role as a Zen teacher. Sometimes couples share an interest in the same spiritual practice, but only one mem-ber chooses to become a teacher or leader, while the other chooses to devote his or her energy to some other aspect of life such as a cre-ative art, career, or home. Sometimes each partner has different spir-itual interests. Whatever the case, each person's spirituality is of primary importance and should not recede into the background.

Each year awards are presented to the Hollywood stars for their performances in the movies, and as we all know, there is a category called best supporting actor. We cannot overestimate the impor-tance of this role in relationships. A relationship depends on a spirit of cooperation, each person with the other, rather than competition. A relationship in which one partner is out front all the time, in all aspects of the couple's life, and the other partner is always in the background providing support, is a relationship out of balance. Each person should be encouraged to step forward in various ways, and each should also learn the supporting role.

One January several years ago, a student of ours invited us to join her and her family for a Chinese New Year celebration at her uni-versity. We met her father, who was visiting from China at the time, her husband, who was a researcher at the university, and her young son, who was dressed in a traditional red silk outfit for the occasion. Hundreds of Chinese men, women, and children and their guests shared a buffet that included many kinds of delicious noodles and dumplings. After the meal there was a variety show on stage in the front of the auditorium. It included both modern and traditional

Chinese music and entertainment. On the program, after the intermission, was listed "Ball Dance." We were expecting some sort of traditional Chinese dance that involved throwing balls back and forth and were surprised when it turned out to be a ballroom dance routine performed by four couples. They were dressed in suits and tea-length dresses, and they waltzed very formally to the music of Brahms' lullaby. Although it seemed somewhat incongruous, it was also quite lovely. They danced so precisely and were so obviously enjoying themselves that it made a memorable impression on us. Dance is a good metaphor for balance in our relationships and in our spiritual lives.

WHEN YOU DANCE FACING A PARTNER, you step back as your partner steps forward. When you step forward, your partner steps back and vice versa, back and forth. When you dance side by side you step forward and backward in unison round and round the floor. Once you have the basic steps down you can add some twirls and style and expression. But the main point is that you enjoy yourself, each other, and the moonlit evening.

Relationship work and spiritual work need to be balanced with a good measure of playfulness. Don't take yourselves too seriously. When the two of us go off to Zen retreats and workshops, we always make sure to work in some fun along the way. When we have long distances to drive, we pack a picnic to eat outside along the way, and we borrow a book on tape from the library. For us, a suspenseful mystery is a way of sharing a common interest while on the road.

Often we plan to arrive early at the retreat center so we have time to take a walk together and wind down. On one trip, as we walked around the grounds we came upon a playground with a big old-fashioned wooden seesaw. We climbed on opposite ends and relaxed in the summer sun as we went up and down, up and down. There are some things you just can't do alone, and riding a seesaw is one of them. The weight and momentum of each balances the other and sets you both into alternating rhythmic motion up into the sky and back down to earth again. There's an element of trust involved in this activity: you have to trust that your partner will not let the end of the plank hit the ground too hard and will work with you to bring yourselves back to a level position before getting off together. This is a great exercise in equality and balance, and it brings some fresh air and playfulness into your relationship. Next time you pass a playground together, try it for yourselves.

RELATIONSHIP IS NOT A THING

Our Zen teacher, Roshi Kennedy, has a beautiful calligraphy prominently displayed on the wall in his zendo. It was a gift Koun Yamada Roshi made for him many years ago in Japan. It says, "Fundamentally not one thing exists."

This is an important Zen concept or, more accurately, Zen *experience*. Zen meditation is a process of emptying out all things, all concepts, all words, all theories, and all images.

Once when Charles was giving an introductory Zen workshop he instructed the group on how to do zazen, and after the first meditation period he asked the participants if they had any questions. Right away a woman raised her hand and asked, "Would it be possible to have some music playing in the background? I felt a little restless and think music would make it easier." He explained that music is not used in Zen meditation. Music evokes images. In this type of meditation we are going beyond thoughts and images no matter how pleasant they may be. Ease or pleasure is not the point. We go beyond the limits of our imagination and open to something larger.

Yet, when you have gone beyond everything you can imagine and everything is emptied out, you will see, as great ancient Zen master Keizan tells us, "There is still something that cannot be emptied." What is it that cannot be emptied out?

It cannot be expressed in words because this something is not a thing. Words describe the relative world of phenomena, cause and effect, and change. But there is something vast, open, boundless, and clear that lies within and beyond the phenomenal world. Although truly we can say nothing about it, many have tried to express it in words. Zen Master Bankei called it the Unborn. Zen Master Hongzhi called it the bright, boundless field. One danger in calling it anything is that in our minds we quickly turn it into a thing—a beautiful and subtle thing perhaps, but still a thing. And thus we limit it.

Relationships are like this too. The quality of a relationship changes when it is lived with an awareness of this vast, unbounded reality that is not a thing. An awakened intimate relationship, like vast unbounded awareness, is expansive, inclusive, and energizing. It gives you the stability, fluidity, and resilience needed to deal with the demands of constant change. It allows you to be fully present and alive with your lover moment by moment, open to unlimited possibilities in your life together.

The first koan many Zen students work on is Mu. It goes like this. A monk asked Zhaozhou, "Does a dog have Buddha nature or not?" Zhaozhou said, "Mu." In Japanese, *mu* means no. Looking at this koan on an intellectual level, it is important to know that Buddha taught that everything, including rocks, plants, and animals has the same essential nature, or Buddha nature. So it does not make sense for Zhaozhou to answer, "No." Zhaozhou's Mu is urging us onward beyond thought and reason to a fuller experience of life. Zhaozhou may be telling us, "No, you are asking the wrong question." Or "No, stop, you are looking in the wrong direction." Or "No, keep going and exhaust all questions and all things."

Zen students meditate on Mu until they can present a clear experience of it to the Zen teacher. If they get stuck anywhere along the way, the teacher points this out and urges them onward, "Go deeper." This koan has the power to breathe new life into you, to shake you up and wake you up, and bring you to your senses.

This koan sheds new light on relationships. First and foremost it helps us see that, in its essential nature, relationship too is not a thing. In order for a relationship to exist two people must *relate* to one another. Relationship is not something that exists independent of relating. On one level this is obvious, yet it is surprisingly easy to lose track of this in practice. *You must relate with your partner moment by moment, day by day, to continuously co-create your relationship.*

A relationship is not something that you "have." It is not something that can be owned, possessed, or attained. Your partner is not a thing that can be owned, possessed, or attained. Relationship is mutual opening to and presence with one another. If you step back into the mentality of "have" or "have not" life is drained out of a relationship. Relationship is life lived together awake, sensitive, and responsive to the needs of one another. When you wake up to the essential nature or sacred nature of your partner, of your relationship, and of everything around you in the world, it transforms your life and way of relating. One man we know has a very strong meditation practice. He meditates every day along with working at his demanding full-time job and spending time with his wife and young children. He plans his time carefully so he can attend several all-day, weekend, and eight-day retreats each year. He loves meditation and at retreats often sits extra periods well into the night. After several years of practice, at the end of a week of intensive meditation, he told us he'd finally seen that although he loved his wife and children he had been viewing them as something that kept him from spiritual practice, that kept him from gaining spiritual insight. As a result he often felt frustrated and discontent. Now he could see that his wife and children were themselves an essential aspect of his spiritual practice and a perfect manifestation of spirit and life itself. He was moved to tears by this insight and said with head lowered, "It was right in front of my face. How could I have missed it all this time?" Then looking up at us he smiled.

He continues to be an avid meditator and to maintain his full-time professional practice, but the quality of the time he spends with his wife and children has changed. His attitude has shifted. He no longer feels torn apart by the false dichotomy he once created within himself between what is and is not spiritually valuable. His demeanor is brighter, and he is able to experience joy in his life just as it is.

Spirituality, like relationship, is not a thing. It is easy to turn "spirituality" or "spiritual development" into a thing—into something you want or something you want more of. Some people set out to have one spiritual experience after another, accumulating them as one would material possessions. This tendency is so widespread that Chogyam Trungpa's book *Cutting Through Spiritual Materialism* has become a classic for our generation.

Spirit, essential nature, and God are not things that can be owned or possessed. They cannot be named or captured by a concept. Nor can love. If you try to place them in a box they lose their power in your life. But if you sit in silence with an open mind, they will be there with you. You will feel a connection. You will see that you are not separate or isolated. You will see that your life itself is a great treasure.

Both spirituality and relationship involve feeling and seeing connection and then living according to this vision. In addition to overemphasizing materialism, our culture has disproportionately emphasized individualism. In many cultures, connection with the earth, plants, animals, family, clan, and tribe is assumed. When a Native American goes out to seek a vision, it is not for his own spiritual development, it is to connect with the power of the Great Spirit and learn something that will help the people. His identity is not separate from the group. Therefore, there is no individual spiritual advancement apart from the increased well-being of the group.

Spirituality is not for you alone. Relationship is not for you alone. Both can bring you home to live in harmony with expanded vision, renewed energy, appreciation for the beauty of life, and love for yourself and others. Your relationship with your partner is a special opportunity to embody spirituality and connection right here and now. If you do not see it here and now and live it out here and now then, in the words of Master Wumen, "Body is lost! Life is lost!" And moreover: Love is lost!

APPRECIATING PARTICULARITY
AND DIFFERENCES

WHEN PEOPLE set out on the spiritual path often they are seeking an experience of unity or oneness. And indeed spiritual traditions such as Zen cultivate the direct experience of oneness—an experience of the undivided essential nature of all things. Other traditions speak in terms of a mystical union with God. Although it is expressed differently, there is a common emphasis on the experience of unity.

As a result, some people fail to see the spiritual value of the multiplicity of beings and experiences. The experience of unity or oneness does not obliterate differences. Paradoxically, it highlights them and gives us a greater appreciation for their particularity, for the relative world of differences. In fact, there is no universal apart from the particular. Our appreciation of the particular, and the particularity of our relationship, is enhanced when we experience it as a unique fleeting manifestation of the universal—here for just this moment.

When people fall in love, they find themselves attracted to one another by both their commonalties and differences. When we first met and became a couple, we were both interested in folk music and spent many evenings gathered around the living room with a group of like-minded friends playing guitars and sharing songs. We were interested in various social causes and volunteered together at a nearby daycare center for migrant workers. We both liked being outside and went hiking and camping together, breathing in the fresh beauty of nature.

We were attracted by our similarities, but also by our differences. Your partner's differences sometimes complement or balance certain of your own characteristics or qualities. Charles is lively and outgoing, conversing and joking, setting others at ease and drawing in a circle of friends. Ellen, by nature, is more serious, studious, quiet, and reserved. These differences not only complement each other, they help us get in touch with and express another side of our own personalities.

In meditation you gain an appreciation for differences in another sense. The periods of attentive quiet, on a regular basis, allow you to get to know yourself more and more completely, and when you do you see that you are absolutely unique. You are the only one who sees the world the way you do. And appreciating this uniqueness in yourself helps you to see it in your partner.

BEING ALONE IN MEDITATION, taking the time to appreciate your unique gifts, may sound selfish or lonely but if you go deeply into this "aloneness" you experience both your absolute oneness and your absolute difference simultaneously. The experience of oneness enables you not only to *tolerate* differences, but also to expect, appreciate, and enjoy them. It allows you to stand on your own two feet as you enter into an intimate relationship with another human being who is different in many ways.

This is not to say that *all* differences enhance a relationship or that you will not encounter irreconcilable differences in some relationships. A partner's unwillingness to seek professional help and refrain from behaviors such as domestic violence, substance abuse, and sexual addiction are irreconcilable differences. Other differences that significantly decrease the quality of the relationship may warrant exploration with a marriage and family therapist to see if some resolution can be reached. However, you will be better able to live with the differences that are an aspect of all relationships. Still, differences do not have to become a big problem in a relationship if they are viewed in an undistorted way. We differ in the kind of love we long for. Sometimes we want what we lack or lacked in the past. We differ in what turns us on and what turns us off. We feel the need for variety and balance in life. Insight into the effect of any of these factors is valuable in understanding yourself and your partner better and in enhancing your relationship.

One time, during a Zen talk, Roshi Kennedy told a story about a game he used to play when he was a toddler. His older sister often took care of him and would sit him up on her lap. She wore a medallion around her neck that had a picture of the Virgin Mary on one side and a religious symbol on the other. He would reach up and turn her medal over and say, "I like it *this* way." She would then turn it back and say, "*I* like it *that* way." And they would continue turning it back and forth repeatedly.

It's not a matter of right or wrong, or of one way or another. It is a simple fact that we all have different likes and preferences, and sometimes that's all there is to it.

Learn to lighten up! Enjoy your differences in good humor, and embrace life in all its variety. Imagine a living room decorated all in one color: the walls, the carpet, and the furniture perfectly matched. It would lack contrast and be quite boring. An accent color here and there can bring it to life. The same is true in a relationship. A relationship with no differences or challenges would be quite dull.

Dealing with differences requires a change in attitude. Sometimes we automatically associate differences with conflict or view differences in terms of right or wrong. But another way to view differences is as an opportunity to expand your horizons and to sometimes try something new. Dealing with the differences between you and your partner is not just a matter of accommodation, it is an adventure and an impetus for growth.

ACCEPTING YOURSELF AND YOUR PARTNER

ACCEPTANCE is crucial to the success of a relationship, and is a key lesson learned from a meditation practice. Awake and attentive, you become aware of aspects of yourself that you had not noticed before or had repressed or denied in some way. You reconnect with the many facets of yourself and open to your unbounded essential nature—your larger self.

Throughout this process, you cultivate an attitude of openness and inclusiveness—not critical judgment and exclusion as is the impulse for many of us! You sit face to face with whatever comes up and do not judge it, try neither to hold on to it nor push it away or deny it. Meditation can be a practice of seeing and accepting yourself completely, just as you are.

There is a powerful Christian hymn called "Just as I Am" that conveys this deep experience of acceptance: "Just as I am, without one plea...oh, Lamb of God, I come, I come." This song touches the depths of total acceptance. It sings out a willingness to come forth, just as you are in this moment, without a single plea—not a single "except for" or "yes, but." You are willing to be completely present with God just as you are right now. Self-acceptance and presence to that which is larger, by whatever name, or by no name, lay the groundwork for accepting your partner. In order to engage in an intimate relationship with another person, both people need to feel free to open up and share both positive and negative feelings and aspects of their lives and personalities. However, there is a deep human fear of rejection, abandonment, and ridicule. Without a trust in your willingness to accept him or her as a worthwhile, lovable human being, regardless of weaknesses and mistakes, your partner will remain defensive and hidden from you. Acceptance is essential for openness and intimacy and is difficult to learn.

On the other hand, we learn about the pain of rejection at an early age. One Christmas, Ellen's mother, who is a doll collector, received a little baby doll whose face was puckered up and his mouth wide open as if crying. She asked our grandson, Matthew, who was five at the time, why he thought the baby was crying. Without hesitation, Matthew said, "Because the kids were teasing him and making fun of him."

When our granddaughter Brenna was only two, one day she stood looking at one of her little baby blankets. On it was a picture of the backs of a teddy bear and bunny who were sitting on a park bench looking off at the sunset. With a look of concern on her face she asked, "Why don't they like me?" We explained that they did like her, but their backs were turned to her because they were looking away to watch the sun going down. She matter-of-factly said, "Oh." She quickly accepted this explanation and happily went on her way. But to hear this from a little girl who had experienced nothing but love in her young life was a good lesson in our sensitivity as human beings to rejection.

A relationship is a safe refuge from the rejection we inevitably experience from time to time in the world. Acceptance nurtures the individual partners and allows a relationship to deepen, grow, and blossom.

An attitude of total acceptance is expressed in a saying of Zen Master Yunmen: "Everyday is a good day." He urges us to let go of the past and, living in the present moment, experience life just as it presents itself.

But Yunmen is not the ultimate Pollyanna. This is not just positive thinking or denial of the real mistakes, losses, pain, tragedies, and difficulties of life. It is an affirmation that life is worth living even though it has its ups and downs. Even a day you or your partner loses a job, is diagnosed with cancer, or is involved in an accident is a "good day" if you are fully present to your life as it is—and respond with all your resources and humanity. The novelist Elizabeth Berg once said, "I think one of the reasons we have children is to believe in everything all over again. And I'm not talking Santa, here, either." The newness and freshness of a newborn baby calls forth our human qualities and our best effort. Each new day, like a new baby, is to be accepted as a gift, fresh and clean. Every baby is a good baby and every day is a good day.

Spirituality is not a self-improvement program. Zen practice is not undertaken to fix yourself or your relationship. It is a way to open to the incredible gift that you have already been given. It helps you realize and be the magnificent human being you already are.

At the same time, acceptance—even of "Every day is a good day"—is not a passive resignation to life as it is. There are many things in the world that call out desperately for change and improvement. Meditation practice helps you come face to face with the things in your own life and in the world that need to be changed. Rather than ignore or deny these problems, we acknowledge them and accept the responsibility to change what we can. We also accept the fact that there are many things that are beyond our control, and so we focus our energies where we can be effective. Acceptance means that no mental energy is used up in denying, resisting, or worrying, and therefore our energy is available for acting to make necessary changes.

You start with accepting responsibility for your own thoughts, feelings, attitudes, behavior, and life. For example sometimes you look at your life and must accept the fact that you are too busy and as a result worn out. You accept the need to simplify and act accordingly. Change flows from accepting the reality of the situation, not from fighting or denying it. When you are no longer in over your head and drowning, you will be better able to extend a helping hand to others.

Many people have trouble accepting the fact that they cannot change another person. You can change yourself, but you cannot change your partner. Do not get into a relationship hoping your partner will change or improve. This is a recipe for disappointment and disaster. A person may change over time, but that is by his or her own choice and initiative. You can inspire change by the positive changes you make in yourself, but nagging or trying to control will only create resistance. Acceptance is the approach that is most likely to encourage change. However, sometimes what you come to accept is that the relationship is not working even though your have given it your best and that it is time to move on.

Acceptance is akin to appreciation—appreciation of yourself, your partner, and life itself. Acceptance brings peace and joy to relationships and life. It is like Walt Whitman's exuberant and expansive "Song of Myself" that reaches out to embrace and celebrate the life going on everywhere. "I celebrate myself...For every atom belonging to me as good belongs to you." Acceptance celebrates and unites.

FREEDOM IN RELATIONSHIP

O FTEN WHAT PEOPLE FEAR most in making a commitment to a long-term relationship is that they will lose their freedom. They fear the relationship will become a cage. Maintaining freedom within the parameters of a committed relationship is a vital issue—so how can you balance autonomy and individuality as well as interdependence and interconnection?

We live in a time and place where we have more freedom, options, and opportunities than ever before in the history of humankind. You are free to choose your career, your partner, your lifestyle, and your religion.

But the freedom to have other sexual partners is a freedom you relinquish with the commitment of a long-term relationship. This is a basic ground rule for fulfilling and lasting relationships. When this rule is violated it can cause harm on multiple levels. Having other sexual partners is physically dangerous to yourself and your partner. Working as a nurse, Ellen has cared for many people who were devastated to find out they had a sexually transmitted disease that their unfaithful and untruthful partner gave to them. Many of these diseases are not curable, and they stay with the innocent partner for life. Long after the affair has ended the physical wounds and scars remain for life, or worse, in the case of AIDS, may even steal away life itself.

If this is not reason enough, consider the psychological and spiritual harm illicit sexual activity inflicts on yourself and your partner. Such betrayal causes great pain to your partner and erodes his or her trust and confidence. It harms rather than helps your partner's well-being. In addition, the person having the affair undermines his or her own character, honesty, and integrity.

Sometimes people associate Buddhist meditation with "crazy wisdom" and think that "anything goes." They think that acting wild and free is a sign of being spiritually advanced. They mistakenly think Zen's iconoclastic approach means that there are no rules. However, Zen and other Buddhist meditation approaches assume that the practitioner's actions are guided by basic precepts of moral and ethical action. It is true that we are all radically free, but we also have rules to play by. Without becoming legalistic or moralistic, we need to do our best to live with integrity.

This is one way that living in relationship can be viewed as a spiritual practice. One modern master, Yamada Roshi, says that self-realization in meditation is only the entrance to our final goal: namely the accomplishment of our character. He goes on to say that "There is really no end to the practice of Zen. You cannot accomplish a perfect character in forty years. Practicing a million years is still insufficient." Honoring your commitment to your partner's well-being and spiritual development, and living with integrity in your life and in your relationship, are spiritual practices that last a lifetime.

In- and outside of meditation, thoughts and feelings may arise about having a physically intimate relationship with someone other than your partner. When they do it is important, as cannot be stressed often enough, to treat these thoughts and feelings with awareness rather than denial or repression. As with other thoughts and feelings you can watch them rise and fall without adding to them or acting on them. If these thoughts and feelings are persistent they show us that there are issues in our primary relationship that need attention. Some of these can be worked out with your partner, and some may require the help of a therapist. Rather than heeding these impulses to infidelity, take them as a call to work seriously on building up your relationship with your partner.

The freedom that is essential in a relationship is the spiritual freedom of each partner. Spirituality is different for each individual, and each person needs to be free to meditate, pray, and /or worship in whatever way is most personally meaningful. This may change over time, and each partner needs to feel free to change suddenly or gradually at his or her own pace. Each person should have the freedom to explore, create, follow an intuitive call, or pursue a dream. This is the kind of freedom that encourages the spiritual development of each individual and allows the spiritual strength of the relationship to grow as well.

There is a Zen verse that can give us a new perspective on freedom in relationship: "When a bird flies, it comes and goes, but there are no traces." Flight conveys the feeling of freedom, of moving through the vast clear sky, with wings outstretched and nothing to weigh you down or obstruct your movement. Leaving no traces, you are just this moment in time and space. When the moment is gone it is gone. This image of no traces is a powerful one and always reminds me of backpacking trips we take into wilderness areas. The backpackers rule is, "Whatever you take in you carry back out with you." No trash is left behind to spoil the original beauty of the environment in its natural state, wild and free. This is the kind of freedom we want in a relationship. Leave no traces so the original beauty of your partner remains unharmed and can shine through, wild and free. As you move through life together, share the present moment. Be free and unencumbered by the past. Move with fluidity and grace. Let nothing linger to mar the clarity of your presence together in each new moment.

This is certainly not easy when a couple has experienced betrayal or breaches of trust earlier in their relationship. However, this is where meditation can be a powerful ally. If one's partner has admitted past mistakes, sought help with the problem, assumed responsibility for past actions, asked for forgiveness, made restitution if appropriate, recommitted to the relationship, and not repeated the offending behavior, then the innocent partner needs to be willing to let go of the past. This does not mean *forget* the past, much less lessons learned. It means a willingness to move into the present. Rather than holding on to the pain of the past or ideas about our partner, come face to face with our actual partner here and now, this moment. Our daily practice of meditation where we moment by moment make the choice to let go of thoughts and come back to just breathing, just sitting, develops our ability to let go of the past and come into the present. With practice we can carry this valuable skill into our relationship where it can have a profoundly healing effect.

What runs counter to freedom is the desire to control. Just as you cannot change another person, you cannot control him or her. Your partner has the freedom to choose you and to choose to live in relationship with you. Although it is a choice you both make when you commit to living your lives together, it is a choice that is renewed each day and each moment.

This choice is like the choice you make from moment to moment in meditation. You make the choice to be present and attentive, or you choose to allow your mind to daydream and drift elsewhere. You choose to be present and alive in your relationship, or you choose to allow yourself to be elsewhere either in body or in mind.

There is a koan about freedom that helps us to see what it is and how to live it.

Once a monk went to Zen Master Jianzhi and said, "I beg the priest in his great compassion to give me the teaching of liberation." Jianzhi responded, "Who is binding you?" The monk said, "No one is binding me." Jianzhi asked, "Then why are you seeking liberation?" With this the monk was awakened.

Neither a Zen master nor your partner can free you. You have to free yourself.

If you are not free, take a good look at yourself and see what it is that is binding you. You cannot blame your partner for your feeling bound.

Sitting in meditation you see that in your heart and mind you are free to view things the way you want to and you are free to tell the story of your life as you choose. You are also free to move beyond your thoughts, views, and stories and open to something new, something vast, unbounded, and ultimately free. You are free to determine how present you are to another person and to life itself. Only you can open your heart to love and feel its freeing power.

When you see and experience this completely, you can drop the final trace, the seeking itself, and move freely in the present moment. In the present moment, you are free to be who you truly are, and you are able to allow your partner the freedom to be who he or she truly is and to choose to share the moment together.

GIVING AND RECEIVING

Relationships flourish when there is a mutual flow of giving and receiving between partners. Meditation is an exercise in receiving. Our attitude during meditation is one of openness and receptivity. Although throughout our lives we have heard that it is more blessed to give than to receive, being able to receive graciously and gracefully is equally important.

When we take time to sit down in meditation, we open ourselves to receive the gift that has already been given: life just as it is. The gift of nonseparation and unboundedness is ours if we allow ourselves to be completely open and undefended. When we learn how to receive, we accept the gift of life itself with appreciation and gratitude.

Learning to receive has great implications for the quality of your relationship. One of the greatest gifts you can give another person is to truly receive that person. To receive another you create space and time for him or her. You welcome him or her and are ready to listen and hear what he or she has to say. You are able to simply be with each other. Most of us need practice in just receiving, just listening, and just being with. This is a spiritual practice you can engage in together.

Several years ago we had a friend who became interested in meditation and jumped into it full-steam ahead at his local Zen center. He was very outgoing, talkative, and interesting. When he started up a conversation with you, he went on and on and it was hard to get away. He was a dynamic organizer and drew many new people to the center to learn how to meditate. One weekend we spent the afternoon with him before a retreat he had organized. He seemed noticeably more settled and relaxed, he conversed but was not overly talkative, and he seemed to be enjoying himself more. During our conversation over dinner, he mentioned that his Zen teacher had suggested that he do "listening practice." We could see he had an astute and creative Zen teacher who was helping him learn the fine art of receiving.

Receiving in this way is in fact a kind of giving, a kind of generosity. This spirit of generosity is essential. It is life-giving. The Buddhist precept, "Do not be stingy," warns us against trying to hold on to what we have and keep it for just ourselves. Greed and selfish desires are seen as causes of suffering. There is a Buddhist term, *dana*, that means voluntary selfless giving. You can give your time, attention, work, wisdom, or wealth. But whatever you give, the giving is something you do of your own free will, and it is selfless. You are not doing it to get something back in return. Often this aspect of dana has been distorted in that sometimes people believe they are somehow "gaining merit" in return for their generosity, as if merit were some sort of spiritual currency. But true dana is selfless—rooted in the realization that there is no separate self. No self, no merit. There is no keeping score.

This is the kind of giving that is needed in your relationship with your partner. With a spirit of generosity, you do loving acts for your partner without keeping a tally of who owes what to whom. This is not to say that there shouldn't be a balance of giving and receiving in each individual and between the two of you. The quality of your relationship depends on reciprocity, mutuality, and balance. But again: There is no keeping score.

From the perspective of Chinese philosophy each individual, whether male or female, contains both feminine *yin* energy and masculine *yang* energy. Yin is associated with receptivity and wisdom and yang is associated with action and compassion. We can think of yin as receiving and yang as giving. This is just one way of viewing the need to balance complementary aspects within yourself and between you and your partner. When you feel the relationship is out of balance with respect to giving and receiving it is necessary to look both within and without. Are you generous to yourself as well as your partner?

But even giving must be in balance. Giving too much in a relationship leads to feelings of exhaustion and resentment. A person in such a situation sometimes reaches the end of the line and says, "I don't have anything more to give." In a relationship in which only one person is giving, or is giving vastly more, the person on the receiving end is not challenged to learn how to function effectively on her or his own, to give, or to grow. When giving and receiving are one-sided, it is ultimately to the detriment of both partners, and the relationship is undermined.

If people feel they are not receiving what they need in their relationship, they have a tendency to view this as some deficit in their partner. However, part of receiving what you need is *asking for it.* You may not have taken the time to sit down and take a good look at yourself and your life and identify exactly what it is you want or need. Feeling your partner is not giving enough may really mean you don't know what you want and don't want to assume the responsibility for figuring it out. The outcome of this is a vague and constant sense of discontent at not getting your needs met in relationship. After figuring out what you want and need, the next step is to ask for it in a respectful, clear, and specific way. It is not fair to expect your partner to read your mind and give you what you want and need, if you yourself don't even know what you want or won't stand up for what you need.

In addition to bringing giving and receiving back into balance in your relationship, you can expand your vision by moving beyond a dualistic view of giving and receiving to see that they are two sides of one coin. Within Zen literature sometimes the metaphor of host and guest is used. The host is your original or essential nature, whereas the guest is a particular manifestation of essential nature in the relative world. From the perspective of essential nature, when the host gives to the guest, host gives to host. When the guest receives from the host, host receives from host. It is the host that gives and the host that receives.

The one who gives and the one who receives are not separate. When you open to this reality, you receive the gift of a life that is full, rich, and undivided. When you reach out your hand to your lover, you find that the hand that gives and the hand that receives are one hand.

DARKNESS AND LIGHT

I T IS IMPORTANT not to idealize yourself, your partner, or your relationship. From the beginning, you need to realize that both darkness and light are present. Meditation is a safe place to become aware of aspects of ourselves we have denied or repressed before they play havoc with our relationships. There is a tendency to deny or repress the parts of ourselves we view as negative or not in keeping with our self-image. Jung called this our *shadow* and described it as both an individual and a collective phenomenon. Thoughts, feelings, and drives such as selfishness, anger, fear, arrogance, control, sexuality, grief, and shame may be repressed and operate outside your conscious awareness. As a result you find yourself speaking and behaving in ways that are harmful to yourself, to your relationships, and to the world.

Lack of awareness allows these thoughts, feelings, and drives to become imbalanced and take on a life of their own. In the open, nonjudgmental atmosphere of meditation, you become aware of hidden aspects of yourself. Sitting in silence, you simply notice them without adding to them or trying to push them away. You sit without judging or denying. In stillness, you are aware of repressed aspects and how they feel, but you do not fuel them or act on them. Over time, the silent awareness of meditation begins to dissolve their grip on you and their undue influence on your life. These aspects or qualities come back into balance, and you are able to reintegrate them back into your life. You become more human and more complete. The energy used to repress or deny the shadow becomes available for living a rich, full life.

Meditation is a helpful way to become more aware of unconscious influences on your life, but some people have had extremely traumatic experiences in their lives or have serious problems that require psychotherapy. Meditation is not a cure-all. However, it is a very valuable way for many individuals and couples to engage in a lifelong process of becoming aware of the profound subtlety and complexity of themselves and their relationships.

There is a chant that is frequently recited in many Zen centers called "The Identity of the Relative and Absolute." It speaks of the darkness and the light, saying,

> *Light is also darkness,*
> *But do not move with it as darkness.*
> *Darkness is light;*
> *Do not see it as light.*
> *Light and darkness are not one, not two*
> *Like the foot before and the foot behind in walking.*

Zen enables you to live with paradox—to live not-one *and* not-two, simultaneously. You experience the identity of the Absolute and the relative and embrace all aspects of yourself. Yet you don't give the shadow free rein. You befriend the shadow, the wild horse, and win its trust and cooperation. You tame it and ride into life with wind in your hair.

Darkness emerges in the relative. It especially comes out when we try to live with one another. We bump into one another and step on each other's toes. This is not only true in intimate relationships, but in all our relationships. We need to be aware of our tendencies toward comparison, competition, jealousy, and aggression. For example, even though you are happy for your partner when he or she accomplishes a goal and receives honor and praise, along with your happiness you may also feel some twinge of sadness or jealousy. Even though you supported your partner in his or her achievement, and perhaps even more so if your efforts and sacrifices were great, your happiness may be accompanied by a shadow of uneasiness. Rather than denying your sad, jealous, or uneasy feelings, or pushing them into the background, if you are aware of them, you are less likely to let them accumulate into a reservoir of toxic resentment. They will be less likely to sneak around in the shadows, letting their presence be known in passive aggression or vague feelings of depression or discontent. Awareness of your feelings may motivate you to search out and nurture your own talents as well as your partner's. When brought into the light, the shadow becomes a teacher.

The person we already are, with all our strengths and limitations, is lovable, and capable of behaving in a loving nurturing way. But in order to manifest this, a lifetime of sifting away the chaff is required to get to the nourishing wheat within. We keep on sifting to get to the heart of the matter in life and in relationships. Back and forth, back and forth, darkness and light—always open, always aware.

SKILLFUL MEANS FOR NURTURING RELATIONSHIPS

RESPECTING EACH OTHER

RESPECT is the foundation of an intimate relationship. Respect means that we honor each other and hold each other in high esteem. It is the relationship equivalent of having positive self-esteem. In an intimate relationship you like your partner and convey your positive regard to him or her. Respect creates a trusting environment where you feel safe to share your thoughts and feelings openly with your partner.

Respect involves consideration for the rights, needs, and feelings of your partner. You honor your partner's individuality and right to be different. You honor the fact that you will see things differently and will not always agree. You respect your partner's privacy and need for time alone. You recognize the unique perspective, ideas, and gifts your partner brings to the relationship.

The word *respect* comes from the Latin word that means "to look." Adding the prefix *re*, it means "to look again." You look again and see your partner in a new light. Respect depends on an awareness of the other. You are aware of your partner's presence and how he or she is feeling. You see and appreciate your partner day by day, moment by moment, as you look and see him or her again, as if for the very first time. Respecting one another is an ongoing process of awareness, fresh appreciation, admiration, and affection.

An attitude of respect is communicated through words, nonverbal expressions, and actions. When someone speaks to you, answer. Don't interrupt. Don't monopolize the conversation and talk too long. It's simple, but sometimes familiarity breeds contempt, and civility goes out the window—to the detriment of all. Often people are very polite on a first date. They know very well what manners are when they are trying to make a good impression. But once the deal is sealed, they think they can dispense with the politeness and considerate behavior. This is one surefire way for romance to be lost in a long-term relationship. On the other hand, renewing respectful attention to each other is a way to bring the romance back to life.

In Zen there is an expression that refers to the process of meditation: "raise the Bodhi mind." It means raise the mind that works for awakening, for the liberation of all. Wake up and experience the mind that is clear, vast, and boundless. This is what we are doing and aspiring toward in our spiritual practice. The idea and feeling of raising up is similar in quality to respect. When you respect your partner, you honor your partner just as he or she is, and this helps your partner grow and develop.

What is absolutely contrary to this quality of raising up, honoring, and respecting is making comments that are put-downs, ridiculing your partner, and demeaning him or her. Of course most of us avoid these things in direct ways, but there are myriad subtle and backhanded ways that dishonoring creeps into our intimate relationships, and these can be heartbreaking. It wounds the spirit. It undermines the spirit and integrity of the person who is putting his or her partner down in addition to damaging the partner's self-esteem and damaging the relationship.

If you find yourself on the receiving end of such slights, you must, without counterattacking, set clear limits on this behavior. Firmly insist on being treated with dignity and respect.

On one of our recent trips, we visited an old friend, Julie, who we hadn't seen in many years. Since we last saw her she had gotten a divorce and had been remarried for five years. Julie was excited to have us meet her new husband, Greg. We arranged to join them for dinner and spent an enjoyable evening together catching up on old news and hearing about Julie and Greg's current interests and activities. Throughout the evening Greg frequently made positive comments about how supportive Julie is, how well she does at her job, how involved she is in contributing to the community, and how much fun they have traveling and doing projects together. This kind of thing bespeaks a deep a loving relationship.

Sometimes people put others down to make up for their own low self-esteem. They cut others down to size so they will feel taller. But deep down, it doesn't work. In the long view we all rise and fall together. We are all interconnected and united.

On several occasions, Ellen's father, Bob, told a story concerning the comedian Joey Brown. Bob worked as an engineer, and sometimes he was away from home for two or three weeks at a time on business trips. On one of his business trips, he stayed at a hotel in Belaire. Each evening he took a walk outside to get some exercise. One evening while on his walk he saw Joey Brown come walking down the sidewalk in the opposite direction. Joey greeted him and asked his name. Each evening thereafter, when they passed on the sidewalk, Joey smiled and said, "Hi, Bob." This simple act left a lasting impression that lives on.

Most people have heard the oft-repeated ancient Zen aphorism "When you meet the Buddha on the Way, kill him!" But this was a teaching for a culture that already revered and even deified the Buddha. In our culture, iconoclasm comes easy. Respect is more challenging. When you meet your partner on the Way, treat him or her with dignity and respect. Realize that you are one, and at the same time, you are individuals with different interests and needs. Although each person's spiritual path is unique, you are partners on the Way, and are here to help each other along. Do not drag down, demean, ignore, or hinder your partner. In your smile, your silence, your actions, and your words raise each other up in honor and affirmation. Greet your partner each new day with respect. When you wake up together in the morning say, "Good morning, love."

BEING TOGETHER

PRESENCE is the essence of relationship. Most evenings the two of us meditate together. We sit silently on our mats and cushions side by side and are present with each other and with the evening. After the hustle and bustle of the day, it's a special time of just being together with no noise or distraction. There is no talking, just a calm, quiet presence. Although it is peaceful, it is also very much alive. It is a living presence with one another.

Spending time together like this gives you the sense that you are not missing your precious life as it passes swiftly by. You slow down enough to really appreciate your life and each other. You are not two ships passing in the night. On a regular basis, you enjoy just being together.

If your attention is elsewhere, you are not able to relate to the person who is right in front of you. In Zen meditation, you learn to be completely present right here and now, not preoccupied with thoughts or daydreams. During meditation, you are not just mentally present, but are aware and attentive with your whole body and mind. Practicing this kind of presence brings energy and vitality to your relationships. With regular meditation practice, you will notice a qualitative difference in your ability to relate to the people in your life.

Being more fully present with your partner greatly enhances the quality of your relationship. When you are present you are open to love. Loving requires you to cultivate the ability to be present. Most of us are very busy people, having learned to do many things, but most of us have not learned how to simply be. That's what Zen meditation is—simply being right here in this very moment. When you are fully present, with no barriers, you see what this very moment is and you see what you are. You open to unboundedness and the possibility of lasting love.

Love goes beyond a brief romance. The twelfth-century Zen master Hongzhi said, "Where there is no romance is the most romantic." He is speaking about experiencing a more complete union. To go beyond romance, does not mean that romance is dispensable. In order to keep your relationship alive, it is important to make the effort to be romantic with one another. We do not neglect attention, affection, flowers, and dancing. Romance is necessary, but not sufficient. Don't stop there.

When you first fall in love, you are interested in every little aspect of your partner. But after the initial honeymoon period is over, you begin to find many of your partner's traits and behaviors irritating rather than interesting. In the romance phase of a relationship, you are happy just to spend time together. If you are washing the dishes together after a meal, you don't really care how your partner performs the task. You just enjoy being together while you get the dishes washed and the food put away.

After the honeymoon is over there is the tendency to move back into a more critical stance, and issues of control emerge. You may find yourself instructing your partner about the "right" way to do the dishes. Charles likes to wash the dishes in an inch or two of soapy water and to consume a minimal amount of water in rinsing them under running water. Ellen likes to use a large dishpan full of very hot sudsy water and to rinse the dishes using copious amounts of water. The challenge comes in not letting your ideas about the right or wrong way to do the dishes or your desire to control things in the kitchen to overshadow the real person who stands before you. After the initial excitement of falling in love passes, if you can still enjoy each other's company while cleaning up after meal together, this is "most romantic."

Throughout your relationship you need to remain open, awake, and present. Love is not a thing. It is not something you attain or possess. Clinging and controlling destroys it. It is not a state. It is not a place you arrive at and stay, once and for all. Loving is moment by moment.

A loving relationship is an ongoing process of being present with and open to one another. This is not just a matter of spending *more* time together. Relationship has to do with the quality of the time you spend together.

It's important that you cultivate an ability to enjoy just being around the house together even though you are engaged in different activities. As you practice being more fully present, you'll discover your partner's presence is a comfort to you, even if you are not directly interacting at the moment. Knowing your partner is nearby makes the world brighter, warmer, and life a little easier. If you aren't experiencing this, don't blame your partner or your relationship, but rather redouble your own practice of presence. Meditation, alone or together, can help. It is important to set aside time to do things

together. When you do, the fact of being together is more important than whatever it is you may be doing or not doing. Be present
to each other during the time you set aside for yourselves as a couple. Talk, laugh, and appreciate each other while you are engaging in
the activity. Even if you are together in a difficult situation such as
discussing challenging issues with your child or caring for an elderly
relative who is ill, you can take comfort in each other's presence and
support. Love is meant to be shared.

One Friday evening, we both went out together to dinner at a
local restaurant. While driving to the restaurant, we talked about
our week at work and about recent news from an old friend. After
being seated, the waitress brought us a menu, and we discussed what
we thought we each might order. When our food arrived we shared
a bite of this and that and commented on the taste of each. Across
the room, I (Charles) noticed a couple sitting at a table for two. The
wife ordered a salad, and the man ordered a full meal. Throughout
the meal, the wife's attention was riveted to a thick novel she read as
she nibbled at her salad. The husband sat and ate a steak and baked
potato all by himself. They didn't look angry; they just didn't interact. They were together in the restaurant that evening, but you could
easily see they were not present to one another. They were mountains
and rivers away from each other. Although this is an extreme example, the point is, when you go out to dinner together, it isn't just to
get something to eat. It is an opportunity to pay attention to one
another, to enjoy and delight in each other's company.

If you and your partner have trouble being present to one another
and enjoying an evening out together, going out to dinner is a perfect

opportunity to practice. This is spiritual practice as much as the time you spend in meditation, and many of the same strategies apply. In meditation, we use the sitting posture and the breath to help us wake up and reconnect with the present moment. During a dinner out with your partner, first set down whatever is occupying your mind. Come into the present moment by making eye contact with your partner, at least as you toast to each other's well-being, and periodically throughout the meal. Since you do not have to be occupied with the details of preparing and serving the meal, your energy and attention can be focused on listening to your partner and on his or her expressions while speaking with you. Let your attention reside in the present with the taste and texture of the food you are eating. When you reach out to touch your partner's hand notice how it feels. Through an awareness of the sight, sound, touch, and taste of the present you will come to your senses and can use this moment to reconnect with your partner.

Even when you are not physically present with one another, you can maintain a presence and connection through phone calls, letters, and email messages. Often when Charles goes off to lead a week-long retreat, I (Ellen) send a package of chocolates or cookies along in his suitcase and tell him to think of me as he eats them. Presence transcends space and time: even when you are apart, you can be present to you partner in your heart. Your heart is unbounded, and in love you are united.

Last year, our friends Jim and Carol decided to spend their fifth anniversary attending a weekend Zen retreat together. They sat silently side by side in the zendo and at meals throughout the weekend. During breaks they sat beside each other in rockers on the porch looking off at the mountains in the distance, or they walked hand in hand down to the river. At the end of the retreat, during our closing circle, Jim said, "All my life I have been going to retreats, but I always went alone. I am so grateful to finally have someone to share them with me." Carol said, "At first I wasn't sure this was the way I wanted to spend our anniversary, but I'm really glad we decided to come. There is a special closeness in sitting together in silence and a depth of spirituality I experienced here this weekend that I never thought I would be able to share with another person." Although they spent the weekend in silence, they were present together, and shared the profound beauty and peace of the weekend with one another.

Sometimes when couples go to Zen retreats they choose to room together, and sometimes they request separate rooms. Some couples are very comfortable together and find it does not distract them from the intensity of a week or weekend of deep meditation practice. Being together during a silent retreat enhances their practice and integrates more naturally with the flow of their everyday life.

Others want the time and space to single-pointedly focus all their energy and attention on meditation practice and the daily schedule. For them, this is a special period of time set aside from their usual life pattern that is free of any other demands. After the retreat ends, each partner and the relationship will reap the benefits of the intensity of their time apart.

This decision is best left up to each couple to determine for themselves.

It is good to give some special attention to reconnecting with your partner after attending a retreat.

Even if you have both attended together, the retreat will have been a unique experience for each of you. Spending some quiet time alone together after the retreat, even if it is only the time you spend in the car driving home, is an opportunity to share with your partner.

If only one of you has attended a retreat, several things can make the transition back to home smoother. If possible the partner remaining at home can create an atmosphere for reconnecting by having the house in order and preparing a meal or snack. As is true when you reunite at the end of a day, do not bring up problems that have come up or things that need fixing until after you have had some time just to be together. A question such as "How was your retreat?" is an invitation for your partner to share some of his or her experiences. When your partner tells you about his or her experiences, listen with openness and sensitivity. Some experiences in meditation are beyond expression in words, or your partner may simply not want to talk about them, so be accepting of this also. Whether you or your partner feels talkative or not, spend some time being together.

Each couple is the expert on their relationship and how it is best nurtured. You may not feel like an expert regarding your own relationship, especially if things are not going well, and we are not suggesting that you may not need professional counseling from time to time. But you are the only ones who know all the details and nuances of your relationship, and you are ultimately the only ones who can decide whether to work on improving it or ending it. This book is an effort to empower couples in their relationship and to help them view their efforts to live in fulfilling relationship as a spiritual practice. Each couple has their own unique way of practicing and being together.

BALANCING FAMILY, WORK, AND PRACTICE

SPIRITUAL PRACTICE requires discipline. You can't just read about it and think about it; you have to *do* it, and doing it takes time. It takes time to meditate, time to sit with a group on a regular basis, and time to attend retreats. Relationship as a spiritual practice also requires time and attention on a daily basis. Balancing both meditation and attention to relationship is not easy, but it is well worth the effort and can lead to an integrated and fulfilling life.

Many people say they don't have the time to meditate. They get up early in the morning to get ready and off to work on time, and by the time they get home in the evening, prepare dinner, and clean up they are too tired to do anything else. In addition to work, many go to school evenings or weekends to advance their careers. This involves both class time and study time. Couples with children spend most evenings and weekends taking the children to their activities such as sports practices, music lessons, and birthday parties. Amid this whirl of activities it is hard to imagine finding time for a spiritual practice; yet some people do find or make time.

Across the street from our home is a little old white clapboard church. When we sit out on our deck we see the people coming and going and hear the choir on warm days when the church windows are open. It's not unusual for church members to spend several hours there on Sunday morning and then to return for a couple more hours Sunday evening. The whole congregation meets again on Wednesday evening for Bible study. On other days, there are various smaller groups that meet, and you can see members mowing the lawn, weeding the flowerbeds, or shoveling snow. It is not just meditation practice that requires time! Any serious spiritual practice calls for a commitment.

One way to make time for your spiritual practice is simply to make it a priority—let go of some of the other things you spend your time on. Learning to let go is a big part of Zen practice. Not allowing yourself to be distracted with your energy going off in all directions is also part of the practice. Focus your attention on what is most important to you. We all have to pick and choose how we want to spend our days and our lives.

Ultimately, doing this requires you to come face to face with your mortality and acknowledge that your time on earth is limited. Reflecting on your use of time helps you gain perspective, and it motivates you to make good use of the time you have. The only time you have for sure is right now. So, if you want a spiritual practice, begin right now. If you want a satisfying relationship with your partner, begin right now. Begin to choose carefully how you spend your time—your life.

Freud said that in order to be mentally healthy a person needs to be able to love and to work. Work is not just an indication of mental health, it is a requirement in the spiritual arena and the arena of relationships as well. Balancing the demands of work in the world with time for work in meditation and relationship is a crucial aspect of your spiritual practice.

Time for spiritual work should be a consideration when you choose a career or job. How many hours per week does the job require? Can you accumulate comp time for extra hours worked? How much vacation time can you get?

For many years Charles worked as a reading teacher in the public schools. He meditated in the morning before school and again in the evening. Every Thursday morning, he got up at four-thirty and drove into the city in time for morning meditation and a meeting with his Zen teacher. He had all summer and school vacations during the year available to attend retreats and Zen training periods.

During the years Ellen worked as a staff nurse, as long as she was willing to work extra weekends, it was possible to trade times with other nurses on the unit in order to get the time off for retreats. Her daily meditation times varied depending on whether she was working day, evening, or night shift. Later on both of us taught at Radford University and were free to travel during weekends, vacations, and summers to study with our Zen teacher, Roshi Kennedy.

Zen practice based on a traditional monastic model requires extensive time away from your partner and children and can put a great strain on a relationship and on family life. Over the past forty years as Zen has taken root in America, gradually Zen communities have begun to explore forms of practice that maintain the intensity of the practice and yet accommodate the typical work schedules and family commitments of their members.

Many centers now allow members to attend retreats on a part-time basis. Many have *ango*, a three-month period of intensified practice, that members can participate in while continuing to go off to work during the day. Members are encouraged to be actively involved in planning the center calendar for the year so the activities and schedule will meet the needs of the membership.

Time is not the only factor involved in finding balance in life. Balance also involves the quality of our attention and our attitude while engaged in all aspects of life. Often we do not spend the time we have with our partner in a satisfying way and may even find ourselves wasting our time together squabbling or wishing we were somewhere else. Viewing relationship as spiritual practice helps improve the quality of the time we spend together. Bringing the same careful attention, awareness, and compassion to our relationship as we do to our meditation practice can transform our relationship and life.

Often we are asked how a person who has a job and a family can maintain an in-depth spiritual practice. We always say, "Where there's a will, there's a way!" But you often need to expand your view of where spiritual practice takes place. It is not just on the meditation cushion, but in daily life as well. It is not just at the meditation center, but also at home and at work. You have to be determined and creative, but it can be done. Practice on your own every day at whatever place and time you can.

One friend of ours teaches kindergarten. While the children are gone for lunch, she goes into the bathroom that is in her classroom, closes the door, and meditates. She says she is a much better teacher during the afternoon as a result. Another friend who is an engineer works long hours on special projects for his company several months during the year and accumulates comp time so he can spend several weeks off attending retreats.

The third part of the equation that needs to be factored in is time with your partner and, if you have them, your children. Your family needs time, energy, and attention on a daily basis and special time set aside for family events and vacations. You need time to relax and have fun together. Often partners and children protect the meditation time of a family member because they experience that Mom or Dad is nicer when she or he meditates. Partners value meditation as a way to relieve stress and promote health, so they will be able to continue to be there for each other. Children come to accept meditation as a part of the normal routine of family life.

One year when our daughter was young, she searched through the whole rack of Father's Day cards. Finally she gave up and said, "You know they have lots of cards for fishing dads and golfing dads, but they don't have any for meditating dads!" She didn't view meditation as any different than any other activity a dad might enjoy. Spiritual practice can be integrated into your family and work life, but like anything else you might enjoy such as football, golf, eating, or shopping, it needs to be kept in balance.

Balancing family, work, and spiritual practice is a great challenge. It is a dynamic and demanding process, but it can be done, one step at a time.

BEYOND SPEECH AND SILENCE

OMMUNICATION is the way you relate to your partner and form a connection, but it is much more than the words you speak to each other. It also includes silence, active listening, and nonverbal behaviors. Although we all learn to communicate quite naturally as we are growing up, we must also make an effort to learn communication skills to help us communicate more effectively and bring us closer to each other in intimate relationship. Even so, communicating with your partner requires more than merely learning skills. It depends on genuine love, respect, equality, and mutual concern for one another. True and deep communication in an intimate relationship can take place only in the context of an attitude of openness, honesty, trust, and acceptance.

Even before you open your mouth, you communicate a multitude of messages. You speak through your gestures, posture, speed, tone, eye contact, and facial expressions. When you sigh and roll your eyes, the message comes through loud and clear. When you help carry in the groceries without being asked, the message also comes through strongly. When your face lights up as your partner enters the room, affection is clearly communicated.

We are aware of only a small portion of the nonverbal messages we are sending, and the remainder is unconscious. Nonverbal behavior often reflects our feelings and intent more accurately than what we say. It is commonly said that actions speak louder than words. For this reason, often we don't believe a person's verbal intentions to change until his or her words are backed up by an actual change in behavior. Our loving regard for our partners must be expressed and experienced directly, beyond thoughts, concepts, and words.

One day Buddha gave a sermon to a large assembly of monks, and he held up a flower and blinked. Out in the crowd, only Maha-kashyapa broke into a smile. Buddha recognized in Kashyapa's smile that he understood the essence of his teachings. The teaching was transmitted not by words, but with simple gestures—holding up a flower, blinking, smiling. The intimacy of Buddha and Mahakashyapa was beyond words and silence, embodied in a simple smile.

Love is embodied; and it is embodied in silence as well as speech. We communicate as much through our silence as through our words. But silence isn't just silence. There are many kinds of silence. There is the silence of listening with open attention to what your partner is saying both verbally and nonverbally. You attend to both the feelings and the content of what your partner is expressing. You listen with empathy to you partner's perspective and experience of life.

You may become silent as a strong feeling wells up within you and moves you so deeply that you cannot speak. You feel it arise and intensify in your body. Sometimes your voice cracks and you become silent until the intensity of the feeling subsides. There are also pauses of reflective silence. During this silence you take time to pull back to think things through before saying anything more. In addition, there may be periods of open peaceful silence as you enjoy the depth of connection you experience while communicating.

Silence can also communicate negative messages. There is the silence of withdrawal, sulking silence, and angry hostile silence. Silence can be warm and embracing, but also cold and cruel.

Silence can be cowardly when there is the need to speak out or to take a stand.

Open, honest communication does not mean that you should always say everything that is on your mind. Each person has a right to privacy and does not need to share every thought or feeling he or she has. There is a Zen verse that says:

> *If you meet a swordsman, you may present a sword;*
> *You should not offer a poem unless you meet a poet.*
> *When you speak to others, say only three-quarters of it;*
> *You should never give the remaining part.*

Speak in a language that the person you are speaking to can understand. When speaking to your partner, consider not only your own need to express yourself, but also your partner's feelings and needs. Communicate truthfully, but always with kindness and respect. Recognize that it is impossible to communicate your deepest essence, but give only "three-quarters." The whole truth of it is simply beyond words.

It is not always easy to communicate clearly. We misinterpret the words and nonverbal messages of others for myriad reasons. It takes time, sensitivity, and effort to become aware of your own and your partner's ways of communicating.

There are different types of communication. Sometimes we just want to express our feelings and be heard. An intimate relationship should provide a safe place for the expression of both negative feelings such as sadness, disappointment, and frustration and positive feelings such as excitement, affection, and appreciation. At other times our communication is aimed at finding a solution to a problem or addressing an issue. This is an opportunity to clarify the problem, open to possible solutions, consider the consequences of each option, and choose a course of action. The need to communicate openly with your partner is ongoing, as new feelings are experienced and new problems arise. There is no final word.

One day a non-Buddhist went to Buddha and asked him, "Aside from speech, aside from silence, what is it?" Buddha just continued to sit unmovingly. The non-Buddhist was instantly awakened. He bowed, thanked Buddha profusely, and then went on his way. Buddha praised his insight.

When your communication, whether by words, actions, or silence takes place with an open awareness of the unbounded essential nature of reality, as it manifests moment by moment, there is freshness, immediacy, and genuine presence in your relating with your partner. It is *just this look*, *just this gesture*, and *just this touch*. This kind of silence can bespeak a deep connection and union that is beyond description. An intimate relationship is an opportunity to embody connection and unity in both your speech and silence.

Recently, our four-year-old granddaughter came over to visit on her way home from preschool. Charles asked her, "What did you do in school today?" She said, "I played and I don't want to say anything more about it." Sometimes that's a pretty good way to explain spiritual practice. "We meditated and we don't want to (can't) say anything more about it." It may also be a good thing to say about your relationship: "We played and we don't want to say anything more about it." Although sometimes not wanting to talk about an experience can be an expression of withdrawal, hostility, or simply not wanting to make the effort to share, it can also be a genuine expression of the feeling that words can't capture the essence of the experience. Trying to talk about it would miss the mark and diminish it. We can talk things to death, but there are still some things that can't be explained. Don't just talk about your life—live it! Your life together is lived out fully in the moment. Although we do our best to communicate, we must also realize that relationships and life itself are so deep, so intimate, and so wonderful, that they are beyond words and silence.

DISAGREEMENT WITHOUT DIVISION

SINCE EACH OF US is unique, in any relationship there will be different points of view and disagreements. Don't imagine an awakened relationship is in all ways perfect or ceaselessly harmonious. An awakened relationship does not deny differences. Conflict is on some level inevitable, and the way a couple deals with it can either strengthen or undermine the relationship. Anywhere people are living or working together disagreements arise.

Once Zen Master Nanquan heard the monks of the east and west halls of the monastery arguing over a cat. Nanquan walked into the midst of them, held up the cat, drew his sword, and said, "If one of you can say a word, I will spare the cat." No one could answer, so Nanquan cut the cat in two.

There has been some debate about this dramatic koan regarding whether Nanquan actually cut the cat in two or if he just gestured as if he were killing the cat, but this is beside the point. The point is that Nanquan cuts through to the heart of the matter and helps us see that when we argue about our different points of view, life is lost. Life slips away while we are lost in arguing. Lost in the right and wrong of argument, the monks completely missed the beauty and companionship of the cat and of each other and the world around them.

You have probably experienced for yourself how the life goes out of you and you feel drained and depressed after a heated argument with your partner. You draw up sides, east and west, and cut the relationship in two. You turn your partner into your enemy and lose your friend and lover. You miss the beauty and companionship of your partner.

In the collection called the *Blue Cliff Record*, the verse to this koan says:

> *Thoughtless the monks of both halls;*
> *Raising dust and smoke,*
> *Out of control.*
> *Fortunately, Nanquan was there;*
> *His deeds squared with his words.*
> *He cut the cat in two*
> *Regardless of who was right,*
> *Who wrong.*

When we argue there is a strong pull to become thoughtless, but meditation and awareness in daily life can open up more options. It is better to deal with disagreements through a thoughtful and respectful discussion. Explain to your partner your feelings, needs, values, and point of view. Be equally ready to listen to your partner's feelings, needs, values, and point of view. In addition, consider what is needed to preserve and build the relationship. If you discuss rather than argue, you get to know yourself and your partner better as you work together to resolve your disagreements. This is a relationship-building process that unites rather than divides, that brings life rather than destroys.

In sixth-century China, the third Zen Ancestor Sengcan is said to have written:

> *If there's a trace of right and wrong,*
> *True-mind is lost, confused, distraught.*

If we get caught up in who is right and who is wrong when we are trying to resolve conflicts with our partner, then the unity of the relationship is lost. Love is lost as we become more and more divided and distraught. The process of resolving disagreements is as important as the decision that is reached. United in dialogue with one another, you may come up with ideas and possibilities you wouldn't think of on your own. However, if your approach is adversarial rather than cooperative, you may find that you get what you want in the short run, but over time competition and negativity erode the relationship and eventually will kill it! You win the battle but lose the war.

Battling raises dust and smoke and can get out of control. Some couples get into the habit of arguing all the time, and some don't just argue, they fight. For some couples, this leads to angry feelings getting out of control. They find themselves saying or doing things they later regret. Although anger is an aspect of being human, we have the choice and responsibility to express anger in safe and appropriate ways. Although your relationship can and should provide a safe place to express feelings such as anger, frustration, and discouragement, you are still responsible for the way you express them. During a disagreement, if you find your anger becoming too intense, take a break, cool down, think things through, and come back later to discuss the issue together when you can again see and appreciate the beauty and companionship of each other.

Meditation can help you calm down and get in touch with your feelings so you can express them effectively. As you sit quietly, just breathing, you become aware of thoughts arising in your mind and you notice feelings arising in your body. You see how feelings such as anger are fueled by your thoughts, your internal dialogue, and the stories you tell yourself. You notice feelings building to some intensity and then dying down again. It is like waves rising and falling in the ocean. Some waves are small, and others are huge and crashing, but regardless of their size, what goes up inevitably comes down again. As your awareness of thoughts and feelings grows, you become less reactive and controlled by them. You are better able to ride them out and let them go without overreacting or blowing things out of proportion.

In Buddhist teachings greed, anger, and ignorance are called the Three Poisons. Dealing with anger in your relationship is a fruitful area for spiritual practice. Rather than speaking or behaving in an angry or aggressive way, take the time in meditation and in daily life to notice what it feels like in your body each time that anger arises. Pay attention to other feelings that accompany the anger such as hurt or fear. Hear what you are saying to yourself and see how your thoughts escalate your angry feelings. Notice what happens when you let go of self-righteous thoughts and fixed opinions about the situation.

Feel the energy of anger and use it to see ever more clearly.

Meditation does not do away with your feelings, and Zen practice is not about suppressing or repressing anything. You do not numb out. In fact you become *more* sensitive and aware of both the joy and pain of life—your own and others. Even after decades of meditation, you still become anxious, angry, excited, happy, or sad as various circumstances come up in life. You experience the full range of human emotion—but an increased awareness of your feelings helps you deal with them better. You learn to let go of thoughts that fan your anger into rage. You don't add suffering to sorrow with thoughts of helplessness or hopelessness. You become more flexible and free to choose how to express your feelings in ways that don't hurt the one you love.

In ancient India, when two monks engaged in a debate, they each raised a flag at the front gate of the monastery to let the community know about the event. The person who lost the debate took down his flag and the flag of the winning party was left flying to declare the victory. One day a monk named Ananda, who had been Buddha's personal attendant until Buddha's death, went to his teacher Mahakashyapa and said, "The World-Honored One transmitted the brocade robe to you. What else did he transmit?" Mahakashyapa called out, "Ananda!" Ananda replied, "Yes, Master!" Mahakashyapa said, "Knock down the flagpole at the gate." With this, Ananda was fully awakened.

Ananda had a brilliant intellect and could probably win most debates or arguments—but life is not limited to winning arguments. Mahakashyapa helped Ananda drop his thoughts, concepts, and dualistic divisions of winning and losing or right and wrong. This is what he meant by "knock down the flagpole": drop your self-centered view of the world and your egotistical need to be right. Drop all dualistic division. Ananda let it all drop and opened to that which is vast and undivided. He moved beyond opposition and separation between self and other, me and you, give and take, right and wrong, and winning and losing.

When Mahakashyapa called out to Ananda, Ananda's "Yes, Master" was his wholehearted response to the situation at hand. His "Yes" was immediate, fresh, and life-affirming. This is the way we want to respond when our partner calls out to us. This affirms our partner, our relationship, and life itself. It does not mean that we agree on everything, but it shows our attentiveness and willingness to work together on the situation at hand.

When you open to this reality, you will see that you are larger than you think. You will be less likely to act small and petty. You will be able to agree to disagree, or disagree without being disagreeable. There is a Zen expression that says, "Buddhas and bodhisattvas do not interfere with one another." Open to your larger self, you can create a relationship large enough to embrace agreement and disagreement.

An awakened relationship is more than right and wrong, beyond resolved or unresolved, beyond perfect and imperfect, beyond agreements and disagreements. Disagreements are like clouds that come and go through the vast sky. If you do not allow them to overshadow the original beauty of your love for each other, you will be able to disagree without division.

NO BLAMING

OFTEN, ON SNOWY DAYS when the schools are closed, we take care of our grandchildren Matthew and Brenna while their parents are at work. One snow day we played outside all morning sledding down the hill by our house and building a snow fort. By afternoon the sun came out and the roads were clear, so we went to get some groceries. On our way home, we swung by Sonic Drive-In to get the kids a treat. They each ordered a hot fudge sundae with whipped cream and a cherry on top.

When we got home, Charles entered the house first and stopped just inside the door to take off his boots. Matthew was right behind him, sundae in hand. Charles cautioned him to slow down because there was some melting snow on the linoleum and it was slippery. Matthew rushed right past Charles and slipped on the wet floor. His sundae flew up into the air and landed upside down on the kitchen floor. He was not hurt, but he was upset about losing his sundae.

Ellen told him she would make him another one since she had all the ingredients on hand. Matthew stood quietly by watching Ellen clean the sundae off the floor. After a moment or two of silence Matthew said, "It's Grandpa's fault." Charles said, "What did I do? I told you to slow down." A few minutes later Matthew repeated, "It's Grandpa's fault." Ellen said, "Why is it Grandpa's fault? I don't think he had anything to do with it." Matthew said, "He should have caught me."

Though sometimes in more subtle ways, this is what adults do too. In relationships we may tend to blame our partner for our own unhappiness or discontent. Rather than assume responsibility for aspects of yourself that you find objectionable or out of balance, you project these qualities onto your partner. This is not to say that your partner may not have some aggravating qualities or behaviors, but that your vision gets blurred, exaggerated and complicated by your blaming and projecting.

Meditation is a way to bring clarity to your vision of yourself, your relationship, and the world around you. There is a koan that is a metaphor for this process. Once in ancient China there was a boy named Wangzhou and a girl named Qiannu who played together as children. As they grew older they hoped that they would be married one day. However, when it came time for Qiannu to be married, her father arranged for her to marry another man. Before the wedding day, Qiannu and Wangzhou ran away to a distant village. There they lived happily as husband and wife for a number of years and had two children.

One day Qiannu told Wangzhou that she had been feeling homesick lately and wondered if perhaps after all these years there might be a possibility of returning home and asking her father's forgiveness. Wangzhou said that he too was feeling homesick and agreed that they should take a trip back home to see if reconciliation was possible. They loaded supplies for the journey along with the two children into a small boat and traveled down the river to their hometown.

When they arrived, Wangzhou suggested that Qiannu stay down by the riverbank while he went to speak with her father. Wangzhou walked up to the house and knocked on the door. When Qiannu's father opened the door, he was surprised to see Wangzhou and told him that the day he left the village Qiannu became ill and had been bedridden all these years. Wangzhou said, "You must be mistaken. She followed me, and we went together to a far-off country. We're married and have two children! Come down to the boat and see for yourself." As the two men started to head down toward the river, the Qiannu who had been in bed all these years and the Qiannu who had been waiting down by the river came walking across the lawn toward each other and merged into one.

The question Zen masters will ask about this story is this: "Qiannu and her soul are separated; which one is the true Qiannu?"

This koan implies that when you are feeling fragmented and torn apart, you are not your real self, your whole self. When you take the time daily to sit down and meditate, over time, you become aware of all different aspects or facets of yourself. You become familiar with the different thoughts, feelings, needs, and internal conflicts that come up day after day. You see that you are large enough to include all these different aspects, qualities, and tendencies without feeling the need to act them all out, to repress them, or to deny any of them by projecting them onto others.

In some ways, we have all had the experience of fragmentation, but ultimately even then you and your soul are not separated. Your life is like a multifaceted jewel, so rich in all its complexity. There is no need for blame.

One of the Ten Grave Precepts in Zen Buddhism is "Not elevating oneself or blaming others." Meditation helps you see into the subtlety of this precept. When you project your faults or imbalances onto others, it is your ego's attempt to protect your self-image. Zen insight reveals that there is no separate self and therefore the image you are attempting to protect is a false image. In the chant called "The Identity of Relative and Absolute" it says, "The relative fits the absolute, as a box and its lid." There is no need to elevate yourself or protect your self-image. Your actual self is a perfect manifestation of essential nature, just as you are this moment. Your life is also just as it is. There is no need for blame.

Self-deprecation also reinforces a separate sense of self and a false self-image. In fact, in a roundabout way, blaming yourself and thinking you're worse than everyone else is also a kind of self-elevation!

Recently the two of us rented a bicycle built for two, and we went riding off with Charles in front and Ellen in back. Round and round the state park we rode under a crisp clear autumn sky. From time to time, especially when we came to a hill, Charles would glance back and say, "Are you pedaling?" And Ellen would say, "Yes, I am. What do you think I'm doing, just sitting back here coasting along?" This is what often happens in the daily life of couples: at times partners get to feeling that they are working too hard and they blame this on something their partner is or isn't doing. At times there may be some reality to this perception, but often it is a distortion. There is an irrational tendency to blame one's partner for how hard it is to make one's way in the everyday world and to maintain a relationship. A bicycle built for two is a fun way to involve your whole body in getting a feel for working together. We found taking turns being up front in charge of steering the bicycle is also a good exercise in cooperative partnership. It can help you see your tendency to not want to take charge or your tendency to blame your partner for being too controlling.

There is a Zen verse that tells us:

> Don't draw another's bow;
> Don't ride another's horse;
> Don't speak of another's faults;
> Don't inquire into another's affairs.

This is good advice for intimate relationships. Because you live so closely with your partner, there is the temptation to get into his or her business and try to run or improve his or her life. Actually, it is only your own life that you can experience and manage. It is impossible to live another's life. Focus on owning and improving your own faults, not your partner's. Ride side by side on your own horse.

Recently the two of us took a walk together on one of our favorite trails down by the New River in southwest Virginia. The rain had combined with melting snow to cause the river to overflow its banks. The floodwater then receded leaving a layer of fresh mud. It glistened there in the sunlight, moist and smooth. In the right place, even mud has its own beauty and enriches the soil.

But there is no need to sling it around.

NOT JUDGING OR CRITICIZING

WHEN WE'RE ABLE to experience the *thusness* of things just as they are, judging is superfluous. Judging always keeps you one step removed from what is. When you judge and criticize you divide the world. You divide your partner into good and bad. You divide yourself. You don't experience life as a whole.

There is a koan that shows us the limitations of our human tendency to judge:

Once Zen Master Fayan pointed to the bamboo blinds. Two monks went over to the windows and rolled them up in exactly the same way. Fayan commented, "One has gained, one has lost."

Hearing this koan, we quickly get caught up in trying to figure out which monk gained and which monk lost. We wonder how Master Fayan came to this conclusion. Which monk is the winner and which is the loser? Which monk did better? Which monk was criticized? Our lives and our relationships can be lost to this kind of dissection.

Our dualistic thoughts—gain and loss, good and bad, like and dislike—are like blinds that block the sunlight and luster of life itself. When we sit down in meditation and let go of thoughts, judgments, and comparisons, the experience of the vast essential nature of all things shines through. When thoughts and judgments don't cover our eyes, our vision is clear.

But we don't stop there. When we get up from meditation and return to daily life, we see each person and thing just as it is without judgments and comparisons. A peach is sweet and juicy, and so is a pear. Without comparison, each can be enjoyed and appreciated in its own right. You can taste the whole universe in each one. Don't allow the wind of thoughts and judgments to separate you from the sweet, juicy taste of life itself.

In your intimate relationship with your partner, see, taste, and experience your partner just as he or she is in this moment. Let your attention be with your partner, not with thoughts, judgments, and comparisons that separate and distance. Judging your partner, and comparing him or her to some imaginary standard or mental image of what a partner should be, keeps you from fully experiencing your partner and your life. Comparison is death, and comparison is killing. It destroys a relationship.

When you don't judge and compare, you come to appreciate and accept yourself with both your strengths and limitations. You can also come to love and respect your partner complete with his or her strengths and limitations. In this climate of love, respect, acceptance, and appreciation, a person is best able to build on his or her strengths. It is a climate of encouragement and building up that is growth promoting—not criticism and picking apart.

ENCOURAGEMENT AND AFFIRMATION ARE MORE EFFECTIVE in helping a partner get in touch with his or her strengths than criticizing or nagging. One of the reasons we seek and form intimate relationships in the first place is so we can mutually give and receive nurturing and support. One of Charles' education professors once told the class of future teachers, "Never criticize or put a child down, the world will do this more than enough. Your job is to build them up." The same is true in an intimate relationship. There is no need for criticism or put-downs. Your job is to affirm and encourage your partner.

Often during the late afternoon meditation period toward the end of a weeklong retreat, Roshi Kennedy would ask one of us to say a few words of encouragement. This was not a full-length Zen lecture, but a brief talk to inspire the group to wake up and keep going, even when the fatigue and sluggishness of late afternoon set in. Encouraging words were to stir up some energy, to evoke, and to call forth the best effort of each person in the meditation hall. In our experience, some artfully constructed and well-delivered words of encouragement were more effective than the traditional *kyosaku* stick in waking folks up and calling them to attention.

A week of intensive Zen practice, waking up before dawn each morning, and following the meditation schedule on into the evening, day after day, shows you that you have more strength and discipline, both physically and mentally, than you think. You are able to get in touch with your spiritual strength, and this brings new resources to your life and relationship.

During meditation, you notice that thoughts come up, and you hear the things you say to yourself. As you let thoughts go, without adding to them, you learn to let go of the critical and judgmental things you say about yourself. You also become aware of the things you tell yourself about your partner and your relationship. When you catch yourself thinking something like, "My partner cares more about the dog than about me," rather than adding to this thought, you let it go, along with the feeling of deprivation it generates. When you begin to think, "This relationship is hopeless," don't rehash the past and add to the story. Let it go and come back to just breathing. When you stop dwelling on the same old negative thoughts that bring you down, there is the possibility of seeing and experiencing something new. There is more energy available to behave in positive ways that renew your relationship with your partner.

Recently, Charles watched from the kitchen as our four-year-old granddaughter sat up at the dining room table, intensely concentrating on writing her name. As she moved the pencil slowly over the paper, she spoke to her hand, and said, "Listen to me. You can do it." With similar determination and encouragement, you can affirm and nurture yourself and your partner, as you build up and strengthen your relationship.

MAKING LOVE

LOVEMAKING is a superb example of living beyond words and silence, beyond discussion and explanation. At its best, it involves a complete integration of body, mind, and spirit. Through lovemaking you come to know yourself, uncovered, naked and whole. You also come to know your partner in body, mind, and spirit. You know and are known, and simultaneously, you open to the mystery and wonder of nonseparation and union. There is a feeling of excitement, freedom, and peace.

Often lovemaking in not experienced in this way, but such a description can open us to this possibility. Expanding your experience of lovemaking involves taking a look at how you view your body, how your lovemaking reflects the depths of your relationship as a whole, and how lovemaking is an aspect of your spiritual practice. The point of spiritual practice is not to accomplish some state of perfection in relationship or in lovemaking, but to wake up to where you are right now and fully appreciate it.

In many spiritual traditions, the body is thought to be worldly and less than spiritual. Sexuality is denied or repressed. As a result, some people who devote themselves to religious life do not develop a healthy, balanced way to express their sexuality. When sexuality is repressed, it can become an obsession or lead to inappropriate behavior harmful to self and others. Buddha's principle of the Middle

Way is helpful in developing a sexuality that is neither repressed nor excessive.

We need to acknowledge that sexuality is an important part of being human and maintain balance in this area of life. Body, mind, and spirit are one. The body is a doorway to spiritual experience. Your body can help free you from the grip and bondage of your rational mind and ego.

Unlike many types of Christian prayer and meditation, the body is an integral part of Zen meditation. Great attention is given to the posture of the body during meditation. The spine is erect in a natural S-shaped curve. The head is balanced straight over the spine, and the chin is slightly tucked. The shoulders are relaxed down and back, and the chest is open. There is a slight forward tilt to the pelvis and the belly is soft and free to rise and fall with the breath.

During meditation your attention is not on your thoughts or on spiritual ideas. Your attention is on your breathing—your belly gently rising and falling. Or your attention is on "just sitting." When your mind wanders off in thought, you let go of the thought and bring your awareness back to your body, just sitting here in this place, in this moment.

When you meditate regularly, you become more aware of both your body and your mind. You become more aware of your sensuality and sexuality. In the silence of meditation you can feel an owl's hoot reverberate throughout your body. You feel the cold morning air turning your cheeks pink and your breath into clouds. You become aware of your sexual energy and how it feels in your body.

It is not just in your genitals, but in your thighs, belly, chest, breasts, fingertips, and every cell of your body.

Zen Master Yunyan says, "The whole body is hand and eye." You touch and see your partner with your whole body, your whole self. Zen practice is not just about seeing the nature of mind! It is also about experiencing the nature of body. Every cell contains the whole body, the whole universe. The mountains, rivers, wind, and rain are your body, breath, and blood.

In Zen we often hear of going beyond your small mind or ego to open to Big Mind. The same is true for body. You go beyond the boundaries of your skin and experience the One Body. Then you are able to make love with this expanded awareness. Just sitting, just breathing, just walking, just making love—love's body awakens.

Your sexuality is not an isolated thing. Sexuality is interrelated with, and influenced by, your thoughts, your state of mind, the environment, culture, other people, and the whole universe. Sex with your partner takes place in the context of your relationship as a whole. If your relationship is loving, and growth promoting, so is your lovemaking. It is not just a physical release, but rather the sharing of love and pleasure, and the expression of a rich, full life.

Lovemaking, like meditation and relationship itself, requires preparation, time, and attention. Before meditation, you prepare the meditation hall. It is clean, uncluttered, and aesthetically arranged. Someone is in charge of placing a fresh flower on the altar and lighting a candle and incense. You set aside uninterrupted time to meditate.

Before lovemaking, you prepare by cleaning and aesthetically grooming your body. The bedroom is uncluttered, and the bed is made with fresh sheets and soft pillows for comfort. A candle, a flower, music, or a massage with scented lotion can add to the sensuality of the experience. You make time for lovemaking and give your partner your full attention. Lovemaking with awareness is itself a spiritual practice.

Making love with awareness does not mean that you stand back as a witness or observer. It means the witness dissolves. There is no observer. You transcend the duality of observer and observed. You close the gap completely. Absolute and relative are one. Body and mind are one. You and your lover are united in "just this" lovemaking.

The best way to drop the observer and become fully present in lovemaking is to allow your attention to be with the physical sensations of the movement of lovemaking, the look in your lover's eye, or skin touching skin. If your mind wanders off in thought or judgment, let go of the thoughts or judgments, and bring your attention back to just lovemaking. It is the same process we use in sitting meditation when we let go of thought and come back to breathing or the sitting posture. It is like walking meditation when we let go of thoughts and come back to just walking—the sensation of the foot coming in contact with the ground or the movement of walking. It takes ongoing practice, but over time you find you become less preoccupied and more and more present in the moment.

Zen Master Dogen was awakened when he heard the phrase "Studying Zen is the dropping off of body and mind." At once he went to his teacher, Rujing, and said, "Body and mind have dropped off." Rujing approved his insight, but Dogen asked his teacher not to approve his insight without reason, because it might just be a temporary ability or glimpse into the nature of reality. Rujing told Dogen that his approval was not without reason, "You have dropped off dropping off."

When you drop off body and mind and experience vast unbounded essential nature, you open to the universal, the Absolute. But Zen does not stop there, lovemaking does not stop there. You then "drop off dropping off" and return to the phenomenal or relative world and experience it as a moment by moment manifestation of essential nature. You see that there is no Absolute apart from the relative. The particular *is* the universal. You do not make love with the universal—you make love with the particular! You do not make love with just anyone, but rather with your particular life partner and love.

You make love with the one you love. You know the particular qualities and aspects that make your partner who he or she is. And your partner knows the details of your being as well. At the same time you see deeply into *who* makes love with *whom*—into the mystery of not knowing. In embracing both the particular and the universal, the light of love shines.

Lovemaking is "just this"—the universal embodied in a particular moment of intimacy.

GRATITUDE AND GENEROSITY

A RELATIONSHIP is best cultivated in an atmosphere of gratitude and generosity. Gratitude is more than appreciation for the good things in your life; it is an appreciation for life itself, even with its ups and downs. Practice being grateful for the opportunity to be alive and don't take it for granted. Practice being grateful that your partner is alive and practice not taking him or her for granted. Gratitude is life-affirming.

The expression of gratitude has a positive effect on both you and your partner. It helps you clearly see and connect with the positive qualities and actions of your partner. It is all too easy to get bogged down with the irritations, aggravations, and problems that tend to grab your attention and take over your relationship. Paying attention to the positive aspects of your partner and your relationship is not just positive thinking or ignorant denial: it is a way to bring the relationship back into balance. Problems are put into perspective and the positive energy of the relationship is available to help you work together to find solutions and remain connected even if you disagree.

Thoughts are important in the chain of cause and effect. Thoughts and words exert a powerful influence on our lives. Dwelling on thoughts such as "I am dissatisfied," "My partner doesn't pay enough attention to me," "This relationship isn't turning out the way I hoped it would," or "I'm really disappointed" reinforces the ego and its sense of separateness and alienation. This not only influences your behavior in overt and covert ways, it colors your whole perception of your life and relationship and obscures your potential for joy.

It is hard to feel appreciative in a global way. To do so requires awareness of the details of life and the many facets of your partner. When you find yourself feeling dissatisfied, bring your awareness into the present moment and notice anything pleasant or interesting in what you are doing or experiencing right now. If you are vacuuming the carpet, perhaps it's the strength of your muscles at work, or the motion of the vacuum cleaner moving back and forth, or the pattern you are creating in the carpet's nap. In a similar way, each day, notice something about your partner that is pleasing or interesting. Perhaps it's a comment about the news, a touch on your shoulder, the scent his or her clothes hanging in the closet, or a cup of coffee together. An awareness of these little things on a daily basis will gradually help cultivate a feeling of appreciation.

Expressing your appreciation can have a very positive effect on your relationship. When you say to your partner, "I like your new haircut," your partner feels noticed, liked, and attractive. When you say, "Thank you for going out to get the bread. That was so thoughtful of you. Now I can have toast with my morning coffee and cereal," your partner feels acknowledged and appreciated, and his or her thoughtfulness is reinforced. When you say, "I love you," your partner feels affirmed, appreciated, loved, and loving. When you say, "I'm glad to be alive with you," both you and your partner are acknowledged and empowered.

There is a particular dialect here in the mountains of southwest Virginia where we live. Sometimes when you do something kind or helpful for another person, instead of saying, "Thank you," that person will say, "I appreciate you." It's a lovely expression because, it not only thanks you for what you did, it also expresses appreciation for your very being. It acknowledges and affirms your qualities of kindness and caring, and it nurtures those qualities in you.

Awareness is the first step toward gratitude. You cannot be grateful for what you do not see or hear. One time during dinner at the end of a Zen retreat, a woman told about how wonderful the retreat had been for her. She said that about halfway through the week, while she was deep in the silent stillness of meditation, she heard a goose honking as it flew by in the sky. Her eyes filled with tears and she said, "It was just so beautiful. It was like my whole life was worth it just to hear that goose. I'm so grateful for meditation and the opportunity to come to a retreat like this." Later in the conversation she said, "How am I going to tell my husband about what this means to me? When I get home, he'll say, 'How was your week?' I'll say, 'It was great!' He'll say, 'What was great about it?' And what will I say? 'I heard a goose!'" We all laughed with her. Life is so beautiful. Why is it so hard to see and express?

One day in Florida, Roshi Kennedy was walking along a peer and came upon a pelican that did not retreat as he approached. He got quite close to the strange-looking bird with its webbed feet and hanging bill. Roshi Kennedy said he looked into the big bird's eyes and saw himself looking back. Essential nature sees essential nature in the eyes of a pelican. When we approach life like this,

this experience of life brings new reverence and appreciation for all beings, both animals and people, and for the whole world around you. It changes the way you look into your lover's eyes and the honor and appreciation you have for him or her.

Once a monk named Qingshui approached Zen Master Caoshan and said, "I am solitary and poor, I beg you, Master please help me to become prosperous." Caoshan said, "Qingshui." Qingshui said, "Yes, Master!" Caoshan said, "You have already drunk three cups of fine wine and still you say that you have not yet moistened your lips."

Actually Qingshui was not a beginner. He was a monk who had already awakened to his essential nature. He engaged Caoshan in a dialogue in order to see if he could refine or expand his own insight. When Qingshui said he was solitary and poor, he was referring to the experience of emptiness—the experience of essential nature or "no thing." Caoshan knew that emptiness was just one aspect of Qingshui's experience and called out to him, "Qingshui!" When Caoshan called Qingshui's name, he drew Qingshui's attention to emptiness, or essential nature, manifesting in the relative world. It manifests in the unique person of Qingshui and in his every action. Each meal he eats, each glass of water he drinks, and each breath he takes is a cup of the finest wine. Caoshan calls us to appreciate all that we are and all that we have. He wakes us up and helps us see that when we experience the underlying unity of all creation, our eyes are opened and we are able to appreciate the uniqueness of each moment, person, and thing. The light of essential nature shines forth in myriad ways. When we appreciate our many blessings our life is rich and abundant and we are filled with gratitude.

This cultivation of gratitude naturally leads to the practice of generosity. Generosity of spirit is essential in a relationship. Learn to see yourself and your partner not as tight-fisted, materially or otherwise, but rather with hands open and extended to help. Learn to provide for your partner's physical, psychological, and spiritual needs as well as your own, and let go of the times you are feeling withholding or lazy. Give *yourself* to your partner, and work to be the best person you can be.

Generosity of spirit means that you are kind and forgiving—but forgiving does not mean that you simply forget, as if nothing happened. You remember, learn from the past, and make needed changes, but you do not hold on to anger or resentment. You do not hold a grudge against your partner. In failing to forgive, you hold your own heart hostage and your partner in bondage. It is constricting, and there is no room for love to grow. Forgiveness is being merciful and compassionate to yourself and your partner. Let go and move on. This gives your love a fresh chance.

There is a prayer of thanksgiving from a hymn by Fred Pratt Green that the two of us often pray together at mealtime:

> *For the wonders that astound us,*
> *for the truths that still confound us,*
> *Most of all, that love has found us—*
> *Thanks be to God.*

TAKING TURNS

I F YOU WANT to live in relationship, you have to learn to take turns. This is true whether you live in a monastery or with your partner. Everything, from food and water to space and time, needs to be shared. Sometimes this necessitates taking turns. Taking turns is a simple idea, but it doesn't always come easy.

Couples have to learn to share and take turns in little ways and big ways every day. Sometimes sharing is difficult because you don't get to be in control or get your way all the time. You have to take turns with the remote control and who gets to choose which TV show to watch. You take turns doing jobs around the house, deciding what to have for dinner, and when each person can use the computer. You have to share and take turns even if you don't always like it.

Taking turns doesn't mean a rigid fifty-fifty. Taking turns is a flowing back and forth—a give and take without keeping score, not a mathematical equation. There are innumerable factors to consider, and it is a delicate balance, moment by moment.

For many years, we took turns going to school. Back and forth, first one of us in school and then the other until we both completed bachelor's, master's, and doctoral degrees as well as various certificates. Most of the time one partner worked to support us while the other went to school. Sometimes we came up with various combinations of part-time work and school. We supported one another as we completed as much schooling as each of us wanted. It is important that each partner have the opportunity to develop his or her mind, talents, and marketable skills. This way each partner can bring more of him or herself to the relationship. You cannot hold your partner back without holding the relationship, and ultimately yourself, back as well.

For many years, we took turns attending meditation retreats. The first twelve-week retreat I (Ellen) attended was during the winter, and Charles could not get time off from his teaching job. So he stayed home and worked while I went off to meditate. During the summer months, we were able to go for extended meditation periods together. When our daughter was young, most of the time I chose to stay home while Charles attended many weeklong sesshin. Later on, we alternated or attended together depending on our work schedules. We supported each other in spiritual development and Zen study just as we did in our other studies, and together we were able to do more than either one of us could have done alone.

We have known many couples who have supported one another in this way. Paul and his wife Peggy live in Manhattan and have two children. We first met them at Roshi Kennedy's zendo in Jersey City. They had just had their first baby, and Peggy was nursing the baby out in the hallway while Paul was in meeting with Roshi Kennedy. We have been with them many times in the years since. One retreat Peggy is there, and the next time Paul is. On special occasions when the community gets together for a celebration, we see them together with their two children who are now happy, well-adjusted young teenagers.

Supporting one another in practice like this does require sacrifice, as all important things do. Taking turns is a sacrifice, but not a hindrance, and turn taking itself can become part of your spiritual practice in relationship. And sometimes a break from each other brings your relationship into perspective and gives you and your relationship some space to grow. What you learn and experience in your practice benefits your partner and children, and the spirit of cooperation you share enriches your life together.

There is a koan called "Zhaozhau's Three Turning Words": Master Zhaozhau said, "Clay Buddhas cannot pass through water; metal Buddhas cannot pass through a furnace; wooden Buddhas cannot pass through fire." Each Buddha has its own unique character and value. This koan calls our attention to impermanence, flexibility, and not having a fixed image of yourself, Buddha, God, or your partner.

If you see through your self-image and self-centered desires, they dissolve as clay in water, metal in a furnace, or wood in a fire—and then divine light illuminates your life. We should not be too set in our ways and become rigid like a statue. A real human being, especially one living in relationship with another, needs to be fluid like water, warm like a furnace, and alive like a dancing flame. Turning words have the power to turn your mind around and shift your perception. Taking turns also has this power. Ultimately, though, ask yourself this: "*Whose* turn is it?"

Each week, the two of us take turns giving the talk at the Wednesday evening meditation of New River Zen Community. Listening to each other give the talk is not just a welcome respite from having to come up with something new to say each week, it is a moment of intimacy and inspiration. It is truly an opportunity to grow in our understanding of each other and of the Dharma.

When it is your turn to talk—or do anything!—step up to the plate and give it your best shot. Take responsibility and act with integrity.

At the time Ellen's grandmother died her sister Kathy was five years old. When Kathy was told that Nana Lucy died, she was quiet for a moment while she thought the matter over, and then said, "Well, she had a good, long turn." Whether your turn is long or short, give it your best. Enjoy it, and live out your life fully.

If you go deeply enough into the question "*Whose* turn is it?" you will realize that in one way or another it is your turn now.

NURTURING YOUR CHILDREN

NURTURING CHILDREN is a wonderful opportunity for spiritual development. You grow as a couple as you share your love for your children, work together to meet their needs, and watch them learn and experience life. Children draw you into the present moment to see the world anew.

Recently our daughter, Clare, and son-in-law, Troy, gave birth to a new baby girl, our granddaughter Elise. Immediately after the birth, Clare remained in the operating and recovery rooms while Elise was brought back to Troy and Clare's room in the birthing unit and placed under a radiant warmer. Troy stood by Elise's side while the nurse checked her over and then left her there to warm up for a while. We sat across the room to allow Troy some time to bond with his new daughter. He was as silent as she was and stood looking at her completely, totally, immediately, and intimately. It was evident from his facial expression and body language that he was not thinking, he was—just looking. He was seeing his new daughter, for himself, for the first time—beyond thought. He had no image or idea about her. He just looked at her lying there new, fresh, unknown, and wonderful! Then he reached out with one finger and gently touched her, stroking up and down her stomach, legs, and feet. He touched her and was touched by her. Just looking and just touching, they were not separated by thought.

Once Zen Master Yunmen said to the assembly of monks, "Look! The world is vast and wide. Why do you put on your robe at the sound of the bell?" Yunmen is urging the monks to take a look for themselves. Look! If you look deeply for yourself, you will be free and see that the world is vast, wide, and unbounded. This kind of looking is not done with just the eyes, but also with ears and whole body and mind. It is looking without ideas or thoughts, without traces. It is looking with the fresh eyes of a child or a new parent.

Yunmen then asked the monks, "If you see that the world is vast and unbounded, and you are completely free, why do you put on your robe when the bell sounds to come into the meditation hall?" This question is not just for the monks; it applies to everyone. Why do you get up in the morning when the alarm clock buzzes? Why do you answer the door when the doorbell rings? Why do you do anything? There are rational answers to many questions, but this *"Why?"* calls us to go beyond rational explanation to see "what is" beyond subject and object.

You don't have to ask new parents, "Why do you get up at night at the sound of the baby crying?" The vast, wide world of motherhood or fatherhood is beyond *"Why?"* When the baby is wet, you put on a clean diaper. There is no thought, there is "just this"—the wonderful working of choiceless freedom. This is love beyond subject and object duality.

> *The baby cries and milk drips from the mother.*
> *Is this one? Is this two?*

Often parents ask how to fit meditation into a schedule when you have children who need care around the clock. One way is for mother and father to take turns watching the children while the other meditates, free of parental responsibility or concern. This provides a needed break, and you return to the children feeling renewed and refreshed.

Another strategy is to incorporate meditation into your daily routine by getting up early to meditate before the children wake up and then meditate again after the children go to bed. Some children have trouble settling down to sleep at a reasonable hour. When our daughter was young, often one of us would take a cushion into her room and meditate sitting on the rug beside her bed while she drifted off to sleep. It was a pleasant part of her bedtime routine and provided a sense of closeness and quiet peaceful transition.

In recent years, on several occasions when we baby-sat our grand-children, we read stories, brushed teeth, and then after tucking the children into bed, we sat in their room and meditated while they settled down and fell asleep. One evening when we were baby-sitting while their parents went to a company Christmas party, we got them all ready for bed and tucked in. As we did, Matthew asked, "Grandpa and Grandma, are you going to *communicate*?" At first we didn't know what he meant. Then he sat up on his bed with his legs crossed and his hands in his lap with his eyes cast down and said, "You know, *communicate*." Charles said, "Oh, you mean *meditate*." Brenna chimed in, "Yeah, meditate. Are you going to meditate in here with us?" This "communication" has now become a cherished tradition in our family.

As the children get older, some families have quiet time. The parents meditate, and the children are free to sit silently with them for a few minutes or quietly read a book for twenty-five minutes. Children benefit from appropriate discipline and structure. Quiet time is a nice balance in the hectic busy lives that parents and children often lead these days. The silence and simplicity of quiet time brings calm relief amidst a whirlwind of soccer practice, music lessons, television, and video games.

NURTURING CHILDREN WE BEGIN TO WONDER, "Who is nurturing whom?" When our daughter was young, she loved to dance, and we took her to many years of dance classes, rehearsals, and performances. While waiting for her, we enjoyed the lively and beautiful music and visited with the other parents. It was enriching for us as well as our daughter. On one occasion Clare was trying to teach me to dance. After half an hour, she became exasperated and said, "Come on Mom, dance with more hips, more hands, more hair!" She knew that you don't just dance with your feet, but with every cell in your body. She was trying to free me up and breathe some new life into me. She taught me to loosen up, lighten up, move more freely, and bring more energy and spontaneity into life and relationships. Children and teenagers can be great teachers. They stop you up short, shake you up, and wake you up. They keep you on your toes and help you regain your sense of humor and playfulness.

MAKING A LIVING

IN LATE EIGHTH-CENTURY China, Baizhang developed rules to guide Zen monastic life. A key aspect of his rule was that every monk, including the abbot, was to spend part of each day working in the fields. Baizhang wanted the monks to work so they didn't have to depend on begging alone to support themselves. Baizhang's emphasis on the value of work helped Zen survive when many other Buddhist sects, the ones that were dependent on donations, died out during years of government persecution. In addition to being an economic benefit, Baizhang's teaching on work was a clear demonstration of nonduality. In his view, the heights of spiritual insight were not separate from everyday labor. His vision can inspire couples, as well as monks, as they strive to make a living.

Your relationship with your life partner is an economic partnership as well as a physical, emotional, and spiritual partnership. One of the developmental tasks of early adulthood is to become financially independent of your family of origin and begin to establish a career. It is best if each partner has the education and skills to support him or herself so your relationship is not based on financial dependence and each can provide income for the couple or family if hard times arise.

One of the principles of Buddha's eightfold path is right livelihood. When you choose a job, you need to consider the effect of the work on yourself, other people, animals, and the environment. You also need to consider the effect of the work on your own spiritual development and that of your partner. Another aspect of right livelihood is your attitude toward your work.

Through your work, you not only support yourself and your family, you make a contribution to society. Any job—be it truck driver, waitress, doctor, nurse, carpenter, secretary, electrician, teacher, or engineer—when done with integrity and excellence is right livelihood. If work is done in a sloppy or careless way, it doesn't matter what the occupation is, it is not right livelihood. Your attitude and demeanor also make a difference. How you do your work is as important as the occupation you select.

One challenge a couple faces is working together to develop a financial plan that meets their needs. How will you come up with the money to pay for food, housing, utilities, phone, transportation, taxes, clothing, and medical care? Health insurance has become a big issue these days. If one of the partner's employers doesn't provide coverage, the couple has to pay a large monthly premium for health insurance. For some couples, this is more than their rent. In addition, the couple has to come up with a plan for saving money for emergencies and for their retirement years.

Financial planning takes a lot of soul searching, open communication, and cooperation. Each partner has to examine his or her goals, dreams, values, and priorities and communicate these to the other. The couple then needs to reach a mutual agreement. This is an ongoing process that is revised as time passes and circumstances change.

Some people think of money and finances as being solely mate-
rialistic and not spiritual. They create a dichotomy between material
versus spiritual. However, if we really engage the nondualistic view
that arises through Zen meditation, this division dissolves along
with all others. The material is spiritual, and the financial decisions
you make are spiritual decisions. How you decide to spend your
money, time, and talents is an expression of your spiritual values.

Meditation is a way to sit in silence and get to know yourself on
a deep level. You get in touch with your talents and creative impulses.
This helps you select a career that is an expression and sharing of
your unique gifts. If you are not able to find a job in the area of your
talents and creativity, you can express your creativity in your leisure
time activities or volunteer work.

Meditation also gets you in touch with your *resistance* to working.
We hope for a job in our area of interest and expertise—work that
is creative and fulfilling. However, often we find we must be willing
to do whatever job is available while working our way toward our
desired line of work. Sometimes the frustration associated with this
reality is projected onto our partner. This is an opportunity for spiritual practice. We can come face to face with "what is," and rather
than blame our partner, acknowledge our own self-centered desire to
avoid the unpleasant, tedious, or difficult realities of many work
situations. When we move beyond our resistance, the difficulty of
work can unite us with all who work hard, and we can labor together.

In fact, it is wonderful to have the capacity and opportunity to
support yourself and your family through your efforts. Some people are disabled and are not able to take care of themselves, let alone

anyone else. Treasure the gift of your ability to work and be of service. To be an ordinary person with an ordinary job is itself extraordinary—if you appreciate your ability to work and make a contribution. Cultivate an ability to work with attention, integrity, appreciation, and a sense of service, and then work becomes an aspect of spiritual practice. Don't imagine spiritual practice ends when you get up off the meditation cushion. It extends throughout your day at home and at work.

If you find yourself drawn to Zen, consider that Zen has its own aesthetic that is simple, natural, and balanced. This aesthetic can inform your financial decision-making. While it is necessary for most people to work to support themselves, time for work needs to be balanced with time for rest, time for meditation, and time to spend with family and friends. One way to accomplish this is to simplify your lifestyle so you and your partner can afford to work fewer hours. A couple needs to discuss their expectations regarding how many hours each partner needs to work outside the home in order to generate the necessary income to cover expenses and savings.

You need to discuss what size house and cars you need versus want and then make decisions together about these major purchases. When you have children, there are multiple factors to consider and balance, such as the cost of daycare, the desire to have one parent at home with the children, and the need for income. Many couples work alternate shifts to maximize the time that at least one parent is at home with the children. The cost of cooking at home versus eating out is another area where you can simplify and save money. Often eating at home allows you to eat a more natural and healthful diet, however it requires additional time and energy for grocery shopping, cooking, and doing the dishes. There are numerous decisions a couple makes each day as they develop and maintain a mutually beneficial and satisfying lifestyle. But don't miss out on the spiritual practice of discussing money with your partner: the process is as important as the outcome!

Financial planning is a sensitive area where there is great potential for control issues to emerge and for feelings to get hurt. Respect for individual differences is paramount. Money and possessions have very different meanings depending on a person's background and life experience: for some people material gifts are expressions of being valued and cherished, and economizing is interpreted as not caring or as withholding affection. Sharing feelings about money issues helps couples understand their different viewpoints and meanings. Equal voice in financial decision-making decreases feeling of being controlled by your partner or budget. Together you manage your money so your financial obligations don't control your time and your life.

Making a living is more than earning money and spending it wisely. It is the way you and your partner take care of yourselves and one another and support the lifestyle and life together you share. The way you make a living has a major impact on your enjoyment and quality of life. It is your way to make a contribution to the wider community in which you live. Making a living should ultimately be an expression of your integrity, spirituality, and love for one another.

WORK PRACTICE AT HOME

TYPICALLY, when you attend a Zen retreat, each morning there is a period of "work practice." Work practice is done in silence, and your attention is kept on your work. Just as you do in sitting and walking meditation, when your mind wanders off in thought or daydreaming, you let go of the thoughts and daydreams and bring your awareness back to the work. Work practice helps you bring the awareness of meditation into daily activities, bringing clarity to all aspects of your life.

At a Zen retreat you don't pick and choose your job. You don't get to say, "I don't like to clean bathrooms. I don't know how to cook. I don't do a good job on windows." The work coordinator either posts a list of assignments or posts a sign-up sheet, and you take what's left when you get a chance to sign up. Everyone helps to the best of their ability with all kinds of work. Over years of involvement in Zen practice, each person becomes capable of doing all the different jobs that are needed to run a Zen center. This not only gets the work done but it builds discipline, competence, and confidence in the members of the community. Everyone works together building a sense of community and mutual support.

Many aspects of this approach may be helpful in getting work done around the house and in sharing household chores equitably. Sometimes this is an area of conflict between couples, with one partner or both feeling that they are doing a disproportionate amount of the work. People often feel taken advantage of, used, unappreciated, or resentful about real or perceived inequities.

Like the work coordinator who draws up and posts a list of work that needs to be done, a couple may find it helpful to make a job list for the home. Some jobs need to be done daily such as breakfast preparation and dishes, lunch preparation and dishes, dinner preparation and dishes, making beds, picking up, and taking out the trash. Other jobs need to be done on a weekly basis, such as cleaning bathrooms, vacuuming and mopping floors, dusting, laundry, grocery shopping, lawnmowing, trimming, weeding, and paying bills. Some work just needs to be done monthly, every several months, or annually, such as changing the oil in the cars, preparing taxes, washing windows, cleaning the garage and basement, organizing closets and cupboards, cleaning the oven, and various home repairs. Of course if a couple chooses to have children or pets the list grows longer. Even small children can be assigned some of the jobs on the list, and their responsibilities can increase as they get older.

A list of jobs creates a visual image of the amount of work that needs to be done, and putting a name next to each job makes clear who is responsible for doing it. The hours each person is employed outside the home needs to be figured into the picture as well. Both partners' participation in composing the list, dividing up the work, and discussing related issues is as valuable as the finished product. Each partner grows in his or her awareness of what the other is contributing and their feelings about the work they are doing. Don't miss the opportunity to express appreciation to one another!

This process has the potential to help a couple simplify or cut back. Many couples are overextended and stressed by the multiple demands of home, work, and family. They are in over their heads. Even with good time management, there are just not enough hours in the day. It is not your partner's fault that you are feeling over-worked, but rather is often the result of unrealistic expectations. The process of listing and discussing jobs opens the door for revising expectations and exploring alternatives. A couple may agree to simplify meal preparation and cleanup by having each person fix his or her own bowl of cereal for breakfast and sandwich for lunch. At dinner they can share a more elaborate meal together.

The Zen center practice of rotating jobs also has value. This cultivates an understanding of what is involved in each task, and it engenders appreciation when someone else does it. Each partner is less likely to feel that the other's job is easier and is less likely to take the work for granted. In addition, exchanging jobs expands your horizons, rounds you out, grounds you, builds your confidence, and prepares you for a perhaps unexpected future.

Don't imagine work is divided into high status and low, lofty and menial, or worthy of time and attention and unworthy. Work practice is a matter of clearly seeing what needs to be done and responding accordingly.

Zen Master Rujing, the teacher of the great Master Dogen, asked his own teacher to make him the sanitation officer at the monastery. His teacher said that Rujing could be the sanitation officer when he answered the question, "How can something be cleaned that has never been soiled?" Rujing looked into this question deeply for over a year. Finally, he returned to his teacher and said, "I have hit upon that which is not soiled." In gratitude for his awakening, Rujing cleaned the toilets at the monastery. With his insight into the unstained nature of all things, he was liberated. He didn't work like a slave, but rather as a person who is completely free. Cleaning toilets was "just this." He simply saw what needed to be done, and he did it, with gratitude. He became well known for cleaning toilets!— and eventually became the abbot of the monastery.

SPIRITUAL PRACTICE SHOWS US how to value the work we do at home as much as the work we do for pay or the work we do at a Zen retreat. No job is beneath us if we are grounded and our eyes are truly open. Each job done attentively and lovingly is spiritual practice.

HOME AS SACRED SPACE

Last winter, a big ice storm blew in suddenly, and our daughter and her family could not get down the dirt road to their home at the lake, so they spent the night at our house in town. The sound of howling winds and sleet pelting against the windows could be heard as Ellen settled our granddaughter Brenna down to sleep on a futon in the room downstairs we use for meditation. As Brenna snuggled under a warm comforter, she said softly, "This house has peace in it."

More important than physical layout and décor is the interpersonal climate in your home. We have all gone into the home of people who are not getting along and felt the icy silence and piercing glares or cutting comments. It makes you feel uneasy and on edge. You want to get out of there as quickly as possible. Many couples turn their homes into a battleground instead of a place of peace, warmth, comfort, and security.

We would all like peace in the world—and the place to start is with yourself. Are you a peaceful person?

There is a koan about a monk who went to Bodhidharma and said, "Your disciple's mind is not yet at peace. I beg you, Master, give it rest." Bodhidharma said, "Bring your mind to me and I will put it to rest." The monk said, "I have searched for the mind but have never been able to find it." Bodhidharma replied, "I have finished putting it to rest for you."

The monk earnestly looks for his mind and what does he see? He sees the same old restless thoughts arising over and over—his conditioned, habitual way of thinking and viewing the world. This koan is encouraging us to sit down and take a good, hard look at this for ourselves. If we do, we see that these ingrained patterns of thought become our same old way of behaving in relationship.

After an exhaustive search, the monk sees that there is no thing to be called *mind*. All thoughts aside, the universe is empty and peaceful. Seeing our restless thoughts for what they are takes ongoing awareness. Seeing beyond thoughts to an openness of mind brings clarity and a fresh, new sense of peace to our life and relationship.

IN MEDITATION, you unclutter and clarify your mind. As you unclutter your mind, you'll find it easier to unclutter your space. As you clarify your mind, you'll find it easier to clarify your priorities.

When you enter most Zen centers you see the clear, uncluttered mind reflected in the environment. As you step through the door, you stop to take off your shoes and place them with everyone else's shoes lined up in neat rows along the wall or on a shoe rack. This is an immediate reminder that you are entering sacred space. It is also a reminder that every place and everything is sacred and even shoes deserve your care and attention.

Most people can greatly improve their home simply by getting rid of the clutter and things they no longer use on a regular basis. Extra clothes and household items can be donated to a local charity. This is a good exercise in letting go and not clinging to things you have outgrown or no longer need. There is a lightness and freedom that comes with letting go. Your home becomes more spacious and relaxing. Also, it is easier to keep clean and organized.

It is helpful to have an area in your home set aside for meditation. It may be a spare bedroom or just a corner of a room. Arrange your mats and cushions on the floor and perhaps a table or shelf with a flower, candle, statue, artwork, or something from nature on it. Keep it simple but attractive so you will be drawn there to meditate each day. You may also want to create a special spot in the garden or on the porch, patio, or deck where you can meditate outside on nice days. This can be a very enlivening experience. Your effort at creating and maintaining a place in your home for meditation makes a statement to yourself and others about what you value and what you find important enough to make space for in your life.

SHARING A NICE MEAL TOGETHER at home is a way for couples and families to become closer. Often we have fresh flowers and candles on the table at mealtime. The other day when our grandson, Matthew, came over and he saw the rose and lighted candle in the middle of the table set for dinner he asked, "Is it a holiday?" Every day is a holy day, and sharing a meal, flower, and candle is a way to increase our awareness of the preciousness and sacredness of life and of the ones we love.

Every room in the house has its own spiritual blessings to share. While in the bathroom, bathe with the awareness that it is a time to relax, cherish yourself, and be refreshed. Don't be lost in thoughts or worries. Let your attention be on the sensation of the warm water washing over your skin, the scent of the soap, and the softness of the towel. Hot running water and a toilet that flushes are great luxuries! Appreciate and enjoy them fully. Don't take them for granted and miss these simple pleasures as you rush through life. The ordinary is truly extraordinary.

Zen meditation leads to an experience of the Absolute—sometimes called "your original dwelling place"—but it doesn't let you to stay there. You must bring this insight back into everyday life in the relative world. When you return to your original dwelling place, you see that your ordinary home is your original dwelling place, as is your body and everywhere else, and you are at home wherever you are. Your original dwelling place is right here. Cherish this sacred space.

MEETING CHALLENGES ALONG THE WAY

BEFORE LOVE ARRIVES

SOME PEOPLE are single by choice, others by circumstance, waiting for the right person to arrive. It's hard to be patient when you are longing for an intimate relationship, but that is what it takes. Ultimately it is better to learn to be content alone while waiting than to rush into a stormy relationship, heartache, and breakup or divorce. Do not deny or ignore the warning signs of trouble ahead, such as addictive or violent behavior; being currently married or on the rebound from a recent divorce; inability to hold a job or serious debt; lack of physical attraction; major differences in values or desired lifestyle; dishonesty or unreliability.

Meditation teaches us the art of waiting. We simply sit down in the present moment, awake and aware of "what is" right here and now. We set aside twenty-five minutes to meditate, and during that time, everything else can wait. Our yearning, storytelling, worrying, and problem solving are set aside. We just breathe. Our concerns about the future are set aside, and we appreciate the present just as it is. We are free to be content with just being alive, just as we are with or without a relationship. This experience can be soothing and may take some of the urgency and pressure out of the search for a partner. We learn to be more open and available so we don't miss opportunities for love when they arrive.

There is a Zen koan about the process of awakening that can be applied to waiting for love to arrive in your life. A monk said to Zen Master Jingquin, "I want to peck from the inside. Would you please tap from the outside?" Jingquin said, "Could you attain life or not?" This koan uses the image of a baby chick breaking out of its shell with the help of its mother. The chick pecks from the inside and at just the right moment, the hen taps with its beak from the outside. The shell breaks apart, and the chick is free to unfold and come to life in the world. This is a metaphor for the Zen student working with the Zen teacher in an effort to break free from the constricting shell of the ego and awaken to a fuller, clearer life—a life that is vibrant, free, and loving.

The time of your awakening is not something you, or your Zen teacher, can control. It takes patient practice day by day. You must wait for the fruit to ripen, and when it does, it falls from the tree. There is no sense in pulling it from the tree before it is ripe. The same is true of the chick. There is no sense in the chick breaking out of its shell until it has developed enough to be viable.

However, patient waiting does not mean inactivity. The chick does its part by pecking. In the case of Zen practice, you do your part by meditating regularly with alertness and attention, by attending sesshin, and by working diligently with your Zen teacher.

With respect to your desire for an intimate relationship in your life, there is much for you to do as you patiently wait. First and foremost, make good use of your time alone! Get to know yourself intimately. Through spiritual practice, get to know yourself better in terms of your thoughts, feelings, values, needs, and desires. Knowledge of who you are in your essential nature and understanding your own unique manifestation in the world will serve you well as you keep your eyes open looking for a possible partner.

Use your time alone to develop your character, interests, and talents. This way you bring more of yourself and more positive qualities to a relationship. Your time alone is a special time when you are completely free to be yourself. Sometimes people are tempted to put up a false front in order to attract a lover, but this is short-sighted. Be yourself. You want a partner who loves you for who you are. Being genuine will lead you in the direction of a relationship that is truthful, open, and whole. Be your best, but don't deny or hide your faults. In balance, both confidence and humility are attractive. As you develop yourself, your life becomes richer, you become more radiant, and people naturally gravitate toward you.

Do what you enjoy. If meditation is important to you, go to a meditation center to meditate, help out, and attend retreats. Often at Roshi Kennedy's Morning Star Zendo, the group meditates together at 6:00 A.M. and then stays afterward for a simple breakfast of coffee, toast, cheese, and fruit. This is an opportunity for people to visit briefly before heading off to work. In addition, people get to know one another as they clean the zendo, help organize retreats, or serve on committees together. Several couples we know met and subsequently married people they met through their Zen practice. If you engage in activities that interest you, you meet people with whom you share common interests.

By getting out and engaging in the activities you enjoy, you become available. However, if you interact with only a close circle of friends while there, you may not be approachable. You need to make an effort to reach out to welcome and interact with new people who attend, as well as the people you have already gotten to know. In this way the circle is always expanding.

While you are waiting for a partner, be compassionate and loving to yourself.

BE A LOVING HUMAN BEING to others. Stay connected with friends and family. Engage in some volunteer activity where you give expression to your love. In addition to expressing your love, you just might be introduced to a friend, or a friend of a friend.

Love, like awakening, sometimes comes when we least expect it. It is like the wind that blows where it will. It can gently caress your skin, or it can knock you off your feet, but it cannot be grasped, controlled, or called up at will.

When you are a loving person, love, which is itself nothing other than your essential nature, manifests. If you find a partner, she or he also is a manifestation of the same loving essential nature. When this insight is a reality for you, even as you wait for a lover, you directly experience that love has already arrived.

IS THIS IT?

THE PERSON you choose for a life partner has a tremendous impact on your life. It is one of the most important decisions you make in life, and it calls for careful consideration. There is the saying, "Love is blind." However, if ever there is a time when you need to see clearly, it is when you are entering into a committed relationship.

The silent awareness of meditation provides an opportunity to step back from the excitement of a new romance and open your eyes to the situation arising in your life. It is a pause that allows you to get your bearings even as you are being swept off your feet. It is a time to listen to the subtler voices within that help you stay true to yourself as you grow closer to another. Meditation helps you learn the openness and vulnerability that are required in an intimate relationship. You let down your defenses and allow another to enter.

Meditation teaches you to slow down and pay attention. Both these skills are helpful as you make the decision about whether a person you are dating is a suitable life partner. There are no set guidelines on this, but one rule of thumb is to go through the seasons together. Spend a year paying attention to each other and learning as much as you can about each other and yourselves as a couple. At many weddings there is a reading from First Corinthians 13:4, "Love is always patient and kind..." This does not just apply after the wedding. It is also applicable before. True love is patient enough to wait and last while you take the time you need to get to know one another.

Only you can make this important decision in your life, but it is wise not to ignore the input you receive from the people in your life who have your best interest at heart. Their opinions are helpful information to consider along with the best reasoning and intuition you can muster.

And yet, absence of major problems is not sufficient for a mutually satisfying relationship. You need to be clear in your mind about what you are looking for in a partner. These criteria are different for each of us, and they need to be considered in light of what you want your life to be like. Does your partner treat you with respect, politeness, and affection? What are your partner's values and spiritual inclinations? Does your partner take care of him- or herself physically, and are you sexually attracted to one another? Are you able to communicate openly, resolve conflicts flexibly, and tolerate differences? What careers do you plan to pursue? Do you agree on the number of children you want? Where do you want to live? How do you get along with your families of origin? Are your lifestyles compatible with one another? Do you have common interests and desire comparable amounts of time alone? Is your partner trustworthy and reliable? Do you have fun together? If a relationship seems more like work than fun, right from the start, this is a red flag. Humor, playfulness, and spontaneity make relationships more joyful as well as lasting.

While it is important to consider these many facets of a potential life partner and long-term relationship, it's important to realize there is no perfect partner or relationship. Do you have confidence in the ability of you and your partner to continue to learn and grow together? At the same time it is essential that you accept your partner just as he or she is right now, with whatever faults or limitations he or she has. Do not enter a relationship expecting to change your partner. Are you happy with your partner and your relationship just as it is?

Major life decisions are sometimes hard to make, and you fear that you will make a mistake. However, you don't want to become so fearful, anxious, and immobilized that you miss the joy of life. Do not limit life to simply right and wrong, correct or mistaken, successful or unsuccessful. And don't ignore karma, the law of cause and effect. Not ignoring cause and effect means that you need to rationally consider the many factors that make a relationship more or less likely to succeed. And at the same time, you need to open to something larger—the underlying unity of life. Viewed in this light, we don't view life in terms of a mistake. We do our best, and our life is "just this." We live it out with grace, integrity, and appreciation whatever our circumstances.

In Robert Frost's poem "The Road Not Taken" he says:

> *Two roads diverged in a wood, and I,*
> *I took the one less traveled by,*
> *And that has made all the difference.*

This is like the point you reach when you are faced with the decision about whether to enter a long-term relationship with a particular person or not. Either way, it is a decision that changes the direction of your life.

The poem "The Identity of Relative and Absolute" says:

If you do not see the Way,

You do not see it even as you walk on it.

Whatever way you decide, it is the Way. It is your way. It is your grace-filled life. Whether you walk along together or just move on— this is it.

ENDING THE RELATIONSHIP

Ending a relationship is rarely easy. Often it is painful and expensive both emotionally and financially. Sometimes people stay for years in unhappy or harmful relationships just to avoid the pain of separating. Sometimes, as in the case of physical abuse, the decision to end the relationship is clear-cut. However, in many cases it's hard for a couple to decide whether to end their relationship or work on improving it. This is a decision only you and your partner can make. Nobody can make it for you, although counseling can be very helpful in resolving ambivalence, in making changes to improve your relationship, or in working through the transition of separation or divorce.

Feeling the need to end a relationship is a difficult situation to be in, and some people feel that there is no good way out. It's like the Zen koan about a man high up in a tree hanging from a branch by his mouth. Neither his hands nor feet can reach a branch. Along comes a passerby and calls up to him, "What is the meaning of Bodhidharma's coming from the west?" If he doesn't answer, he goes against the wish of the questioner. If he answers, he falls and loses his life. How should he respond?

Some might say that the man in the tree should hold on, but how long can you hold on with just your mouth? Others might say he should answer because he is going to die soon anyway. This koan, and all koans—including the koans of real life—cannot be answered by using reasoning or the intellect alone. You have to go beyond words, answers, and meaning to gain a deep intuitive sense of the direction you need to go in your life. This decision is not limited to a consideration of just your own well-being. It is made with consideration for the well-being of all involved. What do you do when you are in a predicament or dilemma? Bring forth all your resources including your intellect, feelings, life experience, input from friends, professional help, and your deepest spiritual insight to help you do the best you can, given the particular circumstances of the situation.

When it is time for a relationship to end, end it with awareness and integrity. Integrity is the honesty to end one relationship before entering into another. Integrity is acknowledging your part in relationship problems rather than placing all the blame on your partner. Integrity is not ending the relationship in a vindictive or vengeful way. When it is time for your relationship to end, work wholeheartedly to end it justly and compassionately. In practical terms this means working earnestly to negotiate an equitable division of your money and property. Often couples do not see eye to eye on this issue. Being compassionate in these circumstances means interacting in a kind and respectful way even amid disagreement.

Ending a relationship is especially difficult and painful if you would like the relationship to continue but your partner wants it to end. This can be an assault to your self-esteem, and the pain of the separation can lead to intense negativity and anger. This is a time to actively take care of yourself, seek the help of a therapist if needed, and treat yourself with great compassion.

You may find it hard to sit down and meditate during this time of transition. But short periods of daily meditation may be helpful in two ways. Some of your meditations will naturally be more peaceful than others and will provide a welcome and much needed respite from your problems. At other times you may be flooded with thoughts and feelings related to your separation or divorce. Simply sitting in the quiet of meditation with these thoughts and feelings without adding to them or pushing them away can help you befriend them and embrace them as aspects of yourself and of being a human being. This helps release their stranglehold on you, decreases the energy consumed by holding them at bay, and gives you a broader perspective on your life and the current situation.

If you are the one who initiated the separation or divorce, you may have mixed feelings, including feelings of guilt and failure. It is important to acknowledge rather than deny these feelings and to learn from them. A good spiritual practice in daily life is paying close attention to being kind and respectful in all your interactions with your ex-partner. This not only helps your partner, who may be in pain and turmoil, but also builds your own character and sense of integrity.

It is essential to remain aware throughout the process so you can learn about yourself and your relationship patterns. The effort spent on ending a relationship appropriately helps you enter future relationships with greater awareness. This way you won't be as likely to repeat the same old mistakes again with a new partner.

With the ending of a relationship, there is always a sense of loss and the need to grieve. Even if the relationship was so bad that all you feel is relief, you grieve for the love you did not receive. Part of ending relationships is doing the necessary grief work and not rushing into another relationship. Often people assuage the painful and lonely feelings of loss and separation by quickly jumping into another relationship. This is a recipe for disaster.

A meditation practice helps you slow down and work through your pain and fear of being alone. The grief and stress associated with the ending of a relationship may cause a host of physical symptoms such as stomach upset, insomnia, fatigue, and muscle tension. This is a time to take extra good care of yourself physically by getting plenty of rest, regular exercise, and good nutrition. Meditation is a way to relax, breathe, and become aware of any tension that is present in your body. Sometimes you notice that you are tensing certain muscles or you are holding or constricting your breathing without having even been aware of it. When you become aware, often you can ease up, let go of the muscle tension, and breathe naturally. This helps restore your physical well-being.

You may notice the tendency to tell yourself the story of the injustice, betrayal, or disappointment you experienced over and over again. Or you may be plagued with distorted thoughts of yourself as a failure. Dwelling on these thoughts can make you feel even worse. This does not mean that you deny or ignore your feelings. Notice them, acknowledge them, and feel them, but don't add to your suffering with endless thoughts, stories, and interpretations. For twenty-five minutes commit to not rehashing the past or worrying about your future. Meditation is a time to take a break from thinking about your problems and just be. In the quiet open space of meditation something new may arise, and a new perspective emerge.

There are many endings in life, large and small. Learning to let go, to feel the pain of separation, to say good-bye, and to move on as a stronger, more mature human being is a valuable lesson to learn. It is a lesson that begins at birth and continues throughout life, and even as we die. Sadness and the pain of separation and loss are a part of life. Although it can be very difficult, you survive and go on to heal and grow.

In Zen meditation you let go each moment as you open to the ever-new present moment. It is a moment-by-moment death and resurrection. In Zen we speak of the sword of Manjushri that cuts off delusive thinking and kills the experience of separation. It is a death-dealing blow to the limited, separate self—yet at the same time this sword brings about new life as a whole human being, undivided and at one with yourself and the universe. The end of your old relationship is the beginning of a new relationship with yourself and with your ex-partner. As your life goes on you may still need to relate to him or her, particularly if you have children. You need to be clear about the boundaries of your new relationship now that you are no longer together. Your new relationship with your ex-partner exists as much in your mind as it does in the external world. If you hold on to your anger, you are held captive by your old relationship. When you let go of your anger, you release yourself from the past. You are free to move into a new relationship with your ex-partner that occupies a much smaller part of your life and consumes far less of your energy. You learn from the past but live in the present. You are free to move on and choose a new partner with greater awareness and wisdom. Wise endings are wise beginnings.

RELATING ACROSS TRADITIONS

OFTEN when we are leading Zen retreats, a person will come in to meet with one of us and say, "My partner is active in his or her own religious tradition but isn't interested in meditation. What should I do?" Others say, "My partner isn't into spirituality at all. What should I do?" The same basic issue emerges in many different forms: How do you deal with spiritual differences in a way that does not create distance or decrease intimacy in your relationship?

The best way to be intimate amid spiritual differences is to talk with your partner about your spiritual experiences and what is most meaningful to you. Of equal importance is listening. Listen with respect, openness, and sensitivity to what your partner finds meaningful and inspiring. In this way, you not only get to know your partner more fully; you take advantage of the potential to be enriched by your partner's spiritual experiences and views.

One day Ellen was discussing spirituality and healing with the nurse practitioner students she teaches. One of the students told the class, "When I was an undergraduate student, I wasn't a spiritual person. I just wasn't. But after I graduated, I got a job in the neonatal intensive care unit. For the past three years I've watched babies take their first breath, I've taken care of babies as they struggled to take each breath, and I've watched some take their last breath. And now I am a spiritual person."

Spiritual development doesn't come just from meditation or belonging to a particular religion, it also comes from life experiences that bring us face to face with life and death. We grow through our daily encounters with other human beings, as we struggle together to meet life's challenges. We experience our shared humanity. Spirituality is different for each of us. For some people, nature is the way they get in touch with their spirituality.

One day a friend, Joe, asked Charles how he could stand to just sit quietly meditating—not moving, not doing anything. He said, "I just couldn't stay still that long. It would drive me nuts." Charles replied, "Well, you go fishing and sit there on the riverbank doing nothing for hour after hour don't you? That's your way of meditating, isn't it? You don't even care if you catch a fish." Joe paused for a moment, smiled, and a peaceful look came over his face. He said, "You know you're right. That is my kind of meditation." He seemed pleased to have his spirituality acknowledged and valued.

It doesn't matter whether you and your partner share the same spiritual path, you can still walk together along the way. One partner may prefer meditation and the other singing in the choir at church. What matters most is that you take the time to communicate with each other about your spiritual experiences and that each of you supports the other in having the time and freedom to pursue spiritual or religious interests. Of course, there is the need to work together on balance, so spiritual and religious activities don't consume an excessive amount of your time and money. Buddha's Middle Way is a useful guideline in this regard.

One woman shared with us that, although her partner does not meditate, he wants her to keep it up. He sees that it's good for her. It helps her handle stress better, and it makes her happier and easier to get along with. When meditation time rolls around her partner says, "Isn't it time for your meditation?" He protects her from interruptions so she has her quiet time each day. One man said his partner doesn't mind sending him off for a weekend retreat because she knows he will come back inspired, refreshed, and more caring.

It is equally important for the meditating partner to acknowledge and affirm the spirituality of the non-meditating partner. Your partner may not have a spiritual practice, but there is something that is most meaningful or inspiring for him or her. Notice and express appreciation for the positive effects of your partner's spirituality on his or her life and on your relationship. Neither person's spirituality is holier or more advanced than the other's. Neither person must or should try to convert the other to his or her way. It's simply a matter of different temperaments and preferences. Each needs the freedom to choose what is best for him or her at each particular time in life. Even though you don't share a meditation practice together, there may be other aspects of your spirituality that you do share in common. You may attend synagogue, church, or mosque together, take a hike in the mountains together, or volunteer in a soup kitchen together.

Interreligious marriages are increasingly common. As a result, an increasing number of people are born into more than one religious tradition. In addition, many people belong to more than one religious tradition by choice. Many of the people we have meditated with over the years consider themselves to be both Jewish and Buddhist. They were born and raised in the Jewish tradition and they see no need to drop their Jewish beliefs or practices in order to meditate and learn from Buddha's teaching. Many have found that meditation and Buddhism have deepened and enriched their understanding and appreciation of their tradition of origin. A scientific and humanistic world-view is a major influence on the spirituality of most people in our culture. While it is now common for people to consider themselves as members of multiple religious traditions, many don't claim to belong to any. A friend of ours, who teaches at the university, once told us about her daughter's frustration in filling out forms that ask for your religious preference. Their family doesn't attend any temple or church. On Sunday morning while most of their neighbors are off at church, they sit around the breakfast table having a big farm breakfast, reading the Sunday paper, and sharing some relaxed quality time together as a family. One Sunday morning, the high-school-age daughter said, "The next time I have to fill out one of those forms that ask for religious preference, I'm going to write in 'pancakes and bacon.'"

We live in a society of diverse religious views, so the ability to relate across multiple religious traditions is a necessary skill at work, in the marketplace, and often at home as well. In the case of one couple among our friends, the husband is Catholic, and the wife is Jewish. Although they have separate faiths and practices that are a major influence in the life of each partner, what they share in common is that each is deeply spiritual. Each admires and appreciates the goodness and wisdom of the other, and they have a spiritually strong relationship. In the case of another couple we know, the husband practices Zen meditation, and the wife practices Vipassana meditation. Even though their meditation paths differ and they go off in different directions for retreats, they meditate together side by side when they are at home, both doing their preferred form of practice, sitting together in silence.

We each experience the ineffable in our own way. In a climate of openness and acceptance, your spiritual experiences, whether the same or different, provide a fresh fertile field in which your relationship can take root, be nourished, grow, and thrive.

IN GOOD TIMES AND BAD

ONE OF THE REASONS for entering into a committed relationship is to be and to have a helpmate when hard times come your way. Hardship comes with many different faces—physical illness, mental illness, accidents, crimes, and natural disasters. Most of us want a partner who we can count on to be there for us in life's darkest hours.

A year ago Ellen's sister was diagnosed with colon cancer. It was shocking news at her age, with her older child still in college and her younger child still at home. As she endured the ordeal of surgery, chemotherapy, and radiation, she feared that she might die before her children were fully raised. She told us that her greatest consolation during this crisis was that her husband reassured her, "Whatever happens, I will be with you right up to the end."

In Buddhism, we often hear about the bodhisattva's vow to continue working for the awakening of all people and of all creation until even the grass itself is enlightened. On the other hand much less emphasis is placed on marriage vows or commitments made to life partners. It is important to acknowledge and empower your relationship by elevating your vows to your partner to the level of the bodhisattva vow, of deeply religious commitments. "I will be here for you right up to the end, until even the grass itself is enlightened."

Once a monk went to Zen Master Dongshan and asked, "Cold and heat descend upon us. How can we avoid them?" Dongshan said, "Why don't you go where there is no cold or heat?" The monk did not know of any place where there is no cold or heat. Dongshan said, "When cold, let it be so cold that it kills you. When hot, let it be so hot that it kills you."

In some ways this koan is straightforward in helping us confront the fact that nobody escapes the challenges and difficulties of human existence. Although this is a simple and obvious reality, we rebel against it, and in our minds we create elaborate schemes and even whole religious systems in order to try to be good enough and pray hard enough to avoid life's horror and tragedies. Yet despite our best efforts, heat and cold descend upon us.

Master Dongshan suggests that we enter into our circumstances completely with all our resources and not separate ourselves from life itself. Living fully in the present moment, we do what the present situation calls for. It is our sense of a separate self who's singled out for suffering that is killed off, and we are strengthened by the experience of uniting with all creation. The heat and cold do not disappear, but we are not separate from them or from the whole of life.

An intellectual understanding of the inevitability of heat and cold, and how best to cope with them, is a helping hand. But to scale the thousand-fathom cliff of heat and cold requires far more than just intellect. We must have the direct insight that we are not separate from heat and cold and thus we are freed up to face life's crises completely—with skin, flesh, bones, and marrow. In the heat and cold of great crisis, we find the God we relied on to save us from hardship—the God we imagined—is far too small and is shattered by our anguish. And yet, in the moonlight, we see something larger—clear, bright, and full of potential. It is not somewhere else. Beyond expression and beyond any name, it has been here all along. Attuned with this expanded vision, we touch what is best within us and are able to help each other along.

But what was hard won is easily lost. We must continue to work hard in our relationships to remain open and awake to this vision and not quickly fall back to sleep. In times of crisis you may remember how precious life is and how much you love your partner, but once your feet are out of the fire, you can quickly grow cold and fail to feel and express your appreciation for one another. Crises can strengthen and unite us, or they can divide us and destroy relationships. They bring out the best and the worst in us. It is very important for a couple to understand this and create a space large enough for each other during a crisis for the expression of both positive and negative feelings. Accept that each of you may respond and cope with crises in very different ways. Know that if you are mutually supportive you can ride out rough waters together even if one is up while the other is down.

Just being aware that people can have very different ways of coping with crisis and loss is helpful. This understanding moves us beyond thinking that there is one right way to feel or cope and increases our acceptance of differences. A partner may want to be there for you but may not be able to provide what you need at all times. Sometimes it is necessary to seek additional help from a support group of people who have experienced a similar crisis. People in the group will be experiencing various stages and ways of coping with the particular crisis you are facing, and some of them may provide the kind of support you need at the time. Some couples find it helpful to attend the group together, and in some situations only one of the partners attends. The best thing partners can do for one another is to listen to each other with sensitivity and acceptance. Even amid the turmoil you can be united and present with one another, come what may.

One of the hardships that couples face is health problems of one or both partners. We can learn a valuable lesson about coping with illness from Zen Master Mazu.

Toward the end of his life, old Master Mazu was seriously ill, so the chief priest of the temple went to visit him and pay his respects. The chief priest asked Mazu, "How do you feel these days?" Mazu replied, "Sun-faced Buddha, Moon-faced Buddha."

In order to begin to understand this koan, it is helpful to know that Sun-faced Buddha is said to have lived for 1800 years, whereas Moon-faced Buddha lived for only one day and one night. Sometimes you may feel great, like you will live forever; at other times, you feel like you will be lucky to just make it through the day or to live through the night to see the light of a new day. Old Master Mazu is teaching you how to be fully alive and present in the moment whatever your circumstances. You may live a long life, or you may die today. Either way, experience every moment of it, and see that both good and bad times are your life itself. Share your whole life with each other, both good times and bad, living out each moment awake and present with one another.

If you live your life fully moment by moment, use all your resources to rise to each challenge, and stand by one another, hard times will unite you not only with your partner, but also with all of humanity, the whole universe, and beyond.

GROWING OLD TOGETHER

Recently we visited a friend of ours at a local rehabilitation center where he was convalescing after an automobile accident. While we were conversing with him in the day room, he introduced us to a little eighty-four-year-old woman who was at the center recuperating from a hip fracture. They had gotten to know each other well during their daily physical therapy sessions. The old woman told us with great anticipation that she would be going home soon. She said, "I want to get home to my darling." It was so sweet and inspiring to hear about their sixty-two-year marriage and to see the delight in her eyes as she spoke of her husband. She was full of spunk and determined to get better, to return home to her husband, and to keep love alive.

This is the spirit of Zen—to live fully, moment by moment, with determination, joy, and love, right up to the end. There is an expression in Zen literature, "grandmother Zen." Usually this phrase is used in a derogatory way to refer to a Zen teacher who is too lenient or tells the students too much. But actually, "grandmother Zen" could be used in a positive way to refer to a Zen teacher who is nurturing and who is a model for the kind of wisdom and endurance that sustains you for the long haul. It is Zen that is vital, fresh, and sensitive, step by step, right up to the end. It is Zen that lasts and helps relationships last. With the determination, kindness, and hard-won wisdom of a grandmother, you move forward, and others are encouraged to move forward too.

When our granddaughter Brenna turned three years old, it was not easy for her to coordinate her little hand and hold up three fingers to indicate her age. Throughout the day, as people asked her how old she was, she'd say, "Three," as she worked at holding her little finger down with her thumb while she held up three fingers. Toward the end of the day she asked in frustration, "Can I go back to two?"

You cannot go back. You cannot go back to your youth. You cannot go back to when you first fell in love. In order to grow old as truly intimate human beings, you need to be fully alive in the present and bring forth the best of what it is to be an awakened forty-, fifty-, eighty-, or ninety-year-old. Become intimate with what it means to be in a relationship for thirty, forty, fifty, or sixty years. Such a relationship is a rare treasure. A spiritual practice, like Zen meditation, can help you explore its depths and appreciate its beauty.

THERE IS A ZEN SAYING, "On a gnarled old branch, a plum blossom blooms." Just like an old plum tree, an old person or couple can still experience and manifest something new and beautiful. This image brings to mind the old Navajo couple we encountered out in the Arizona desert many years ago sitting side by side in the pinon firelight. They touched our hearts with that which is ancient and sparked in us a new vision of living a deeply spiritual life as a couple. Now grandparents ourselves, we, like the old Navajo couple, are enjoying the beauty and wisdom of growing old together amongst the people as we bear witness to this magnificent possibility.

The Dharma, relationships, and life itself are infinitely profound and subtle. They cannot be exhausted. And so, with patience and practice, spiritual insight and relationship can continue to unfold.

FOR AS LONG AS WE BOTH SHALL LIVE

WHEN YOU MAKE a lifetime vow to one another, within that vow is the recognition that one of you will someday die and the other will be left to mourn and build a new life for him- or herself. Buddhist teachings on change and impermanence can help prepare you for that day, but the actual experience of the reality of the loss of a life partner defies description and is unique for each person.

No amount of spiritual development can take away the pain of loss. In response to the death of his friend Lazarus, the Bible tells us "Jesus wept." Even the most spiritually advanced feel the sadness, grief, and anguish of losing someone they love. The normal human grief response is felt in every aspect of your life, manifesting in physical, emotional, behavioral, and spiritual symptoms that can shake you to the core and bring you to your knees for a period of time. A spiritual practice will not remove this human response to loss. In fact, you may even be more sensitive and feel the pain of loss more acutely.

Where daily meditation and spiritual practice are most helpful is in the gradual rebuilding process that comes after the first several months of intense reaction to losing the love of your life. During this time you continue to honor your partner and what you learned from each other in the past, while you let go of your old life and open to your new life in the present. Your partner will always be a part of your life and can be a positive influence on how you choose to spend your remaining years. The process of adjusting to the death of your partner, while creating a new life for yourself, takes more than time. It takes courage, hard work, and insight. It is a process that is unique for each person.

Recently, our friend's husband died after spending years in a nursing home with Alzheimer's disease. Every day, year after year, even though he no longer recognized her, she visited him and made sure he was receiving good care. For her, the brunt of the loss was felt years ago when his confusion became evident and the diagnosis was made. Her grief was felt again with each successive decline. She said that at the time of his death she felt a sense of release. At the same time, she grieved for all he had been through, for the years of life together that were lost to illness, and for an ending to his life that was different from what she had always imagined. Her family, friends, and spirituality were a comfort to her as she laid her husband to rest, reflected on the life they shared, and prepared to enter a new phase of her life.

Consider this koan: Many years ago in China, Emperor Suzong studied with Zen Master Huizhong, the National Teacher. When Huizhong was very old, the emperor went to him and asked, "When you are a hundred years old, what shall I do for you?" Huizhong answered, "Make a seamless monument for this old monk." The emperor asked, "What style is it to be?" Huizhong remained silent for a while and then he said, "Do you understand?" The emperor said, "No, I do not." Huizhong told the emperor that he had a Dharma successor named Danyuan and he encouraged the emperor to continue his Zen studies with Danyuan after his death.

The emperor was a great benefactor and supporter of Huizhong, as well as being his Zen student. The emperor wanted to build a memorial to Huizhong and wanted his input about the matter. Huizhong was not just interested in the emperor as a benefactor. He was concerned about the emperor as a human being and student, and he worked right up to his death to promote the emperor's spiritual development. Huizhong wanted the emperor to take another step on his spiritual journey, so he did not respond to the emperor's question on a material level.

When Huizhong said, "Make a seamless monument for this old monk," he was saying that the best way for the emperor to honor him was to continue with his spiritual practice. Huizhong used the image of a seamless monument to evoke the experience of nonseparation. But the emperor didn't get it. He remained on the material level and asked about the style of the pagoda. Hearing this, Huizhong knew that the emperor did not understand that he was asking him to *make himself* into a seamless memorial rather than merely erecting a structure of wood and stone. If the emperor had seen clearly, he would have known that the only style he could possibly be is his own unique style, just as he is. In experiencing his essential nature, the emperor would be more fully himself and, at the same time, seamlessly united with everything else.

If throughout your relationship with your partner you are each committed to your own and your partner's well-being and spiritual development, then your dying wish for your partner will be like Huizhong's wish for the emperor. You want your partner to keep going and keep developing spiritually. Connecting with your partner's parting wish for you can be a guiding light as you face the challenges of grief and mourning.

Even for an emperor who already has power and money and respect, the experience of essential nature is magnificent and liberating. Huizhong's dying wish is for the emperor to keep going and one day awaken to the relationship beyond the comings and goings of birth and death. Ultimately, you and your partner are united in both life and death, and so when your partner dies you do not need to suffer in separation. You do not need to wait for a future reunion. You are one right here and now. But again, Zen is not about repression of feelings or about denial, and this does not mean that you will not miss your deceased partner in the everyday world. A unique and precious manifestation is gone forever, and the loss is real. But at the same time, there is an experience of unity and completeness.

At a retreat years ago, Ellen gave a talk on a koan about a monk who asked Zhaozhou, "What is the meaning of the patriarch's coming from the West?" Zhaozhou replied, "The oak tree there in the garden." The monk was asking Zhaozhou about the essence of Zen. Zhaozhou did not reply in an abstract way about essential nature or the Absolute. Instead, he pointed to one particular manifestation of essential nature in the relative world close at hand. He wanted the monk to see that there is no Absolute apart from the relative.

It is "just this" oak tree. "Just this" man or woman you love. "Just this" moment together. We do not love and appreciate essential nature apart from its manifestation in the relative world. It is known and loved in the particular—in your own life and your own partner. Zhaozhou doesn't just say generically, "Tree." He points out the majestic old oak tree standing in the garden outside his door. After the talk, a retired physician came up to Ellen with tears in his eyes, and said, "Your talk about Zhaozhou's oak tree hit the nail on the head for me." He told how he had worked amid life and death all his life, and thought he had come to terms with it. But his wife died several months prior to the retreat, and he never knew how much he would miss her. He said, "I miss her terribly. My wife was so special. She was my oak tree in the garden."

BEYOND THE TWO OF YOU

INTERCONNECTION

Y OUR RELATIONSHIP with your partner takes place within a vast web of relationships. Everything in the phenomenal world is interdependent and influenced by everything else. Your relationship does not just depend on you two. It is influenced in thousands of ways by other people, the environment, and events throughout the world. A spiritual practice such as Zen meditation can help you open to this larger picture of complex interrelationships and provide stability through a direct experience of wholeness. Awareness of wholeness, oneness, or unity, even as it manifests in a multiplicity of relationships, gives you the flexibility and wisdom to nurture your own relationship as well as relate effectively beyond your relationship.

The love you manifest in your relationship with your partner not only influences you and your partner, it has the potency to extend to the ends of the universe and influence the whole world. It is easy to see your interconnection and interdependence in the physical world. When a person, industry, or community pollutes the air or water, everyone suffers the ill effects, even innocent babies and future generations. Although less concretely evident, the same is true in the realm of interpersonal influences. You can see that your wise and loving actions enhance your relationship with your partner, but you may never know all the ways a loving relationship with your partner ripples outward to influence others and sow seeds of love in the world.

Even if you have a wonderful partner and relationship, one of the reasons your relationship is successful is that you have realized that you and your partner cannot rely on each other to meet all of each other's needs. *Interdependence* does not mean that each partner is *dependent* on the other. Each partner needs to be independent as well as dependent. You cannot depend entirely on your partner to meet each and every one of your needs and make you happy. You need to assume responsibility for meeting some of your own needs, while your partner meets some of your needs, and you maintain a network of family, friends, and community resources to meet other needs. If you depend exclusively on your partner and your relationship to meet all of your needs, the well may quickly run dry. But if you reach within yourself, to your partner, as well as to others in the world around you, there is a vast reservoir of assistance and nurture available.

ONE OF THE THREE TREASURES IN BUDDHISM is *sangha*, or community. As individuals and as couples, we need to realize the importance of community. It is a vehicle for both giving and receiving assistance. You depend on sangha to support and help you, and sangha depends on you. Although you and your partner are sangha to each other, it is simply not enough. As a couple, you need to be connected to a whole network of other people, communities, and organizations. You are not separate and isolated.

Zen Master Songyuan asks us, "Why is it that the crimson lines of a clearly enlightened person never cease to flow?" Some suggest that the phrase "crimson line" refers to attachments in the relative world, and others suggest that the phrase refers to the bloodline or lineage of Dharma transmission. So the question is "Why do the attachments of an enlightened person never cease to flow?" and at the same time "Why does the Dharma transmission bloodline of the enlightened person never cease to flow?"

RECENTLY, as Charles was holding our new granddaughter, Elise, he noticed her umbilical cord that had not yet fallen off. It brought to mind "the crimson line," and Songyuan's turning word came to life before his eyes. "Why is it that the umbilical cord of an enlightened person never ceases to flow?" From the perspective of essential nature, there is no separate self and no umbilical cord to clamp off and cut. In our essential nature, we are not cut off and separate, we are one. We can never sever our connection with others.

In the relative, everything is relationship. There is no way for the flow of relationship to cease. Even though the umbilical cord is cut, the love between mother and child does not cease to flow. Like this, the enlightened person does not cut off the flow of loving relationships with others. When you realize your connection to everyone and everything else, you are better able to work toward harmonious relationships, not only with your partner, but also with other people and the great earth itself. There is a Taize song Sensei Anna Gamma taught us many years ago when we attended an interreligious dialogue conference at Lassalle-Haus in Switzerland. She translated it as

> Our human calling is to relate heaven and earth,
> Our human calling is to relate. Alleluia!

Everything is interconnected. The way you relate with others and the world around you brings harmony and beauty to life, or increases suffering and strife. The love you share with your partner is not yours alone—its influence extends throughout space and time.

PULLING TOGETHER

WHEN WE FIRST fall in love, everything is wonderful, and when we first awaken to the direct experience of essential nature, everything is wonderful. But we don't stop there. The spirit of cooperation and mutual support a couple develops to maintain a loving relationship over time is even more wonderful. When the spirit of cooperation and mutual support cultivated by a long-term relationship is joined with the goodwill of others to benefit the community, it is not only wonderful; it is amazing.

As a couple when you work in a cooperative partnership, you can, of course, accomplish more together than either of you could accomplish alone. What is true for a couple is true for a community. Together, you can accomplish more than you can accomplish alone, and you enjoy the support of others along the way.

Spiritual awakening is wonderful, but it is just the first step. There is a well-known Zen koan that asks, "How will you step forward from the top of a hundred-foot pole?" No matter how wonderful a spiritual experience may be, don't get stuck there. Keep going to actualize your insight in daily life to benefit your own life and the lives of others. The action that manifests your spiritual insight, and enriches life, is even more amazing than the insight alone. When your insight helps you join with other hearts and hands to work together to help the earth and all beings, it is most amazing of all.

Collaboration and cooperation don't always come naturally or easily when we have been raised in a highly individualistic and competitive culture. In our drive for self-preservation and advancement, often we try to control or manipulate others to accomplish our goals, rather than join with them to work for the common good. We fail to elicit the collaboration and assistance of others, and as a result, we don't bring out the best in ourselves, or bring out the best in others. Although individual development is important, it can be undermined if we are out of balance and become too self-centered, competitive, or controlling. If our vision becomes too narrow, we become isolated, cut off, and constricted. Neither the individual nor the group benefits.

Meditation helps expand your vision. When you sit in zazen, you do not hold on to any fixed viewpoint. You open to "what is" in all its complexity and immediacy. You become aware of your connection with others and with the whole wide world. You are no longer separate and isolated. Your vision is broad, vast and unbounded. It takes regular meditation, on an ongoing basis, to develop and nurture the wisdom and expanded vision that brings new balance to your life.

WHEN WE LIVED OUT ON THE NAVAJO RESERVATION, each year the teachers and aids at the school worked together on fund-raisers and arranged a field trip to Phoenix for the first-graders. We chartered a bus, drove to Phoenix, visited the zoo and mall, ate in restaurants, and spent the night in a motel. Most of the children had never been off the reservation before and had never seen an elevator or a bathtub. Many of the words in their reading books made more sense to them after their trip to the city. As the bus headed homeward, one little boy said with eyes wide, "Let's go to the world!" Indeed, let us all go to the world together. There is a koan in which Zen Master Lianhua holds up his staff and asks the monks, "When, in olden times, a man reached the state of enlightenment, why did he not remain there?" No one answered, so the master said, "Because it is of no use in the course of life."

If you do not actualize your vision in daily life, what use is it to yourself or others? Likewise, when a couple experiences love and connection, don't let your world fold up and let the connection stop there. Go on to unite with others, be of use in the course of life.

Even though geese mate for life, they continue to migrate with the flock. They join in the V-shaped formation and fly through the sky northward and southward with the seasons. They are not separate from the other geese or from life itself. The spiritual path does not set you apart, nor is it a resting-place. You keep on going united in the flow of life.

On snowy days when our grandchildren come to visit, we all get bundled up and go out sledding on the hill beside our house. Several neighbor kids join us as well. We get everyone all lined up on the toboggan and point out to the gang that there is no steering wheel. The only way to get the toboggan to go where you want it to go is to all lean to the left if you want it to go left and all lean to the right if you want to go right. When we try this out on our way down the hill, the children are amazed that leaning in unison to one side or the other actually works.

Often it feels like life in our world is careening downhill at break-neck speed, on a collision course, out of control, with no steering mechanism, and everyone is leaning in a different direction. We live in constant threat of wars, epidemics, and ecological disasters. Any one of us alone is powerless to avert these crises. But together, we can exert enough of an influence to make a difference. When we pull ourselves together and join with others to keep life going in a positive direction, it is most amazing of all.

SERVANT OF THE SERVANT

WHEN ROSHI KENNEDY first spoke to Charles about his plans to make him a Zen teacher, Charles replied, "It's enough just to be the servant of the servant." He had been traveling around the country to various places with Roshi Kennedy for many years helping him give Zen retreats and often serving in the role of head monk. The head monk maintains order in the meditation hall and takes care of the practical details of the sesshin so the Zen teacher is freed up to put all his energy into meditating and teaching. The head monk and the Zen teacher play off one another to create Zen drama, with the head monk being the disciplinarian and the teacher being the emancipator. There is a lot of camaraderie in working together like this, and Charles truly enjoyed the opportunity to serve, learn, and grow in this capacity.

Years later, when Roshi Kennedy considered Charles's training to be complete, he began the process of making him a Zen teacher in his own right. As is traditional at this time, Roshi Kennedy gave Charles a Dharma name, a Buddhist name chosen by the teacher that is related to some characteristic the teacher has observed in the student during their years of work together. The name Roshi Kennedy chose for Charles was Shinkai. It means "Servant of the Servant."

For a long-term relationship to survive, each partner needs to be willing to serve the other. Often this means doing simple, menial chores like mopping the kitchen floor, driving your partner home from the hospital, picking up the dry cleaning, or fixing the toilet. You serve each other so you are each servant of the servant.

The idea of being a servant is very much in keeping with a spiritual practice such as Zen meditation. When we sit in meditation, we move beyond the bonds of egotistical delusions and open to what is vast and boundless. Being a servant cultivates humility and puts the ego in its proper place. The point of your actions is to be of service, and no task is considered too lowly for the true servant. We see that it is thought, judgment, and comparison that makes some work higher or lower and makes people more or less worthy. Humility makes us teachable and reachable. Arrogance cuts us off from others and from ourselves. Humility is particularly important in an intimate relationship, where it gives partners equal footing on common ground.

In his book about the golden age of Zen in China, John Wu tells a story about Zen Master Chuhui Zhenji on the day he was installed as abbot. On this occasion a monk asked the new abbot, "I hear that when Shakyamuni Buddha began his public life, a golden lotus sprang from the earth. Today at the inauguration of Your Reverence, what auspicious sign may we expect?" Chuhui Zhenji replied, "I have just swept away the snow before the gate."

The monk is expecting the abbot to manifest some special power as a sign of his advanced spiritual development. But no auspicious sign appears, and nothing flowery flows from the new abbot's mouth. Instead, he points to a simple, menial act of service. "I have just swept away the snow before the gate."

This winter we had more snow than usual down here in south-west Virginia. Often when Ellen went out in the morning to get into her car and drive off to work, she found that Charles had swept the snow off the car and scraped the ice off the windshield. This act of humble service is an expression of the kind of love that lasts and is in it for the long haul. This is the eye and heart of the servant.

Sweeping away the snow from in front of the gate also means sweeping away thoughts and delusions that block your entry into a larger, unbounded experience of reality. Scraping the ice from the windshield, your vision becomes clear. The abbot had been sweeping for many years and had swept away everything. Sweeping away every-thing, what is it that remains? What remains cannot be described, but it is a direct experience that can sustain a life of service. This abbot is the kind of person you want to help you see deeply. Not clinging to thoughts, opinions, or ego, with clear unobstructed vision, he is a humble servant who sweeps the new fallen snow from in front of the gate and clears the way for everyone to enter. This is the per-son you want to serve you as abbot and the person you want to serve.

There is a koan in which Zen Master Wuzu says, "Even Shakya-muni and Maitreya are servants of that one. Just tell me, who is that one?" Shakyamuni is the historical Buddha, and Maitreya is a future Buddha, so this koan is telling us that all the Buddhas of the past and all the Buddhas of the future—in fact, everyone—is a servant of that one. "Who is that one?" This koan is a challenge to look for yourself, beyond thoughts and words, and see who that one is. You need to see for yourself, not with just your eyes, but with your skin, flesh, bones, and marrow. Take the time to meditate and inquire deeply, and you will see that the servant and the one who is served are one.

Selfless service does not mean that you become a martyr or a door-mat, or that you work yourself to the bone and become burned out. Selfless service means that your service is not aimed at enhancing your ego. It means that in addition to serving your partner and others, you also serve yourself without being self-serving. You care for your physical, emotional, and spiritual needs knowing that you will not be as effective in helping others if you do not maintain your own health, energy, and inspiration. Taking care of yourself and serving your own needs is another way to be the servant of the Servant.

In selfless service you are united with the people you serve along-side, as well as the people you serve. Engaging with your partner in work that is of service to people in need, or to the earth and all beings, is a way to strengthen your relationship and feel a deep sense of unity with each other, with all of humanity, and with the world around you.

Last year for Father's Day, I bought Charles a new hoe with a lifetime guarantee. It was something he had mentioned wanting. In his weekly Zen talk, Charles mentioned this gift. He said, "I like the hoe, but even more, I like the confidence Ellen has in me. I like the lifetime guarantee!" He joked that the hoe was my way of suggest-ing that he hoe and weed the bushes around the house. He said, "That's just fine. I grew up on a farm. I love digging the weeds, loosening the soil, planting the seeds, and having beautiful flowers grow." On this special occasion, a golden lotus did not spring from the earth, but an attitude of service continued to flourish.

OCEAN OF COMPASSION

THE DHARMA NAME Roshi Kennedy chose for Ellen is Jikai, "Ocean of Compassion." Compassion allows you to be a loving presence with another in both times of pain and times of joy. Compassion is kindness, helpfulness, understanding, acceptance, and love.

It takes a whole ocean of compassion to make it through some of life's toughest challenges and to help others make it through. The ocean is vast, unbounded, and deep. This begins with compassion for yourself, and extends out to your partner, family, friends, and to all beings and the great earth. You need the depth, fluidity, and dynamic energy of the ocean to sustain a life of compassion.

During a recent winter ango, or practice period, Roshi Wendy Egyoku Nakao, Abbot of the Zen Center of Los Angeles, said, "When 'you' die of a broken heart, Great Love arises. Do not fear the tenderness. Great Love is open, vulnerable, and willing to be wounded over and over again." This is the kind of love Zen practice uncovers. Great Love is already here within and all around you. During meditation you let go of thoughts, images, stories, and opinions and discover that you are not separate from life itself. The separate "you" dissolves, and Great Love is free to flow in your relationships and life.

Your willingness to remain tender, open, and vulnerable is essential in an intimate relationship. Otherwise, if you are constricted, clinging, or defensive, the flow of love in your relationship is cut off. Not only do you need to be willing to be wounded over and over again, but you also need to be willing to forgive over and over again. Let go of slights, grudges, and resentment, moment by moment, before love is covered over by them and ceases to light your way. Lay down the past and come to your partner with fresh love and tender affection. Forgiveness is an act of compassion that frees both you and your partner to love again.

An ocean of compassion and love brings joy to your life and relationship. People are naturally drawn to the ocean with its rhythmic waves and warm sandy beaches. They swim in its waters and delight in its constant change. Connecting with the ocean of compassion and wisdom provides a vast reservoir of vitality, blessing, and joy to keep your relationship afloat in both happy times and sad. If you can recognize that you are both the ocean and the wave, you won't lose your bearings by identifying with only the wave. As the ocean, your relationship is larger than the waves of conflict or difficulty that you encounter in life. Your relationship can become an expression of vast love and joy. When you open to this reality, you and your partner are glad to be alive and grateful to be awake enough to fully appreciate each other.

Sometimes people get to feeling that their relationship is in a rut and going nowhere. One snowy Saturday our son-in-law, Troy, called and asked Charles to help him pick up a chest of drawers that had arrived at the furniture store. When they got down to the house at the lake with the chest in the back of the pickup, they got stuck in the snow and ice. The truck wheels just spun when Troy stepped on the gas, and they quickly dug a rut in the snow. Charles looked over at Troy and was surprised to see that he did not seem at all worried. Then, Troy reached over and put the truck into four-wheel drive, and they immediately moved forward.

Meditation can be like four-wheel drive on the road of life. Rather than spinning your wheels in the same old rut, the same old thoughts and feelings, you get in touch with something larger and you move forward. Your way of viewing yourself, your relationship, and the world expands, and you are no longer stuck. You open to new vitality and new possibilities for love. You are free to love.

Love is large. It is not bound. It is not limited. It cannot be measured. It is vast and open like the ocean or the sky.

Yet love is not a thing. So what is love when love is not a thing?

What do *you* love? *Who* do you love enough not to turn into a thing?

What does love look like?

Love is like the wind. Although it can be experienced deep in your heart, and it has the power to unite heart to heart, no one can describe it adequately or grasp it and hold on to it. But you can reach out and hold the hand of the person closest to you. Love is not an abstraction. It is experienced and expressed in the particular—a touch, words of affection, an act of kindness, a meal shared, a smile, a slow dance, an understanding glance. You and your lover can rest in love's embrace and arise refreshed, to see the world through eyes of wisdom and reach out with hands of compassion.

CO-CREATING UNLIMITED POSSIBILITIES

THERE ARE MANY WAYS to be a couple and support one another on the spiritual path. Your love for one another can be expressed in an infinite number of ways. Moment by moment you and your partner co-create your relationship and life. Partnership is a joint venture, or you might say a shared adventure. The journey is not all mapped out in advance, but rather continually unfolds as you go along.

Relationship is a creative process. As in any other creative process, you need to be open not just to your intellect but also to your intuition, spontaneity, ingenuity, and spirit. Creativity is playful, artistic, and expressive. Viewing your relationship as an opportunity to co-create infuses it with renewed energy, enthusiasm, and enjoyment.

Some people view relationships developmentally, with certain expected stages or phases, such as a romance phase, followed by a phase of conflict and learning to deal with conflict that eventually leads to a phase of mature love. Others view the stages of a long-term relationship or marriage as paralleling the life cycle. For example, developmental theorist Evelyn Duvall's eight stages of the family life cycle begins with being a married couple without children and progresses to being a child-bearing family, family with preschool-age children, family with school-age children, family with teenagers, family launching young adults, middle-aged family, and aging family. Each stage presents characteristic developmental tasks and challenges for a couple. While there is certainly some usefulness to these ideas, don't let your relationship become boxed in by them.

Zen presents another view of stages and phases. Once Zen Master Qingyuan went to his teacher and asked, "What should I do so as not to land in some class or stage?" His teacher asked, "What have you done so far?" Qingyuan replied, "I have not even tried the four holy truths." His teacher asked, "In what stage will you end up?" Qingyuan said, "If I still have not tried the holy truths, what stage can there be?"

Vast, unbounded essential nature is indivisible. From the perspective of oneness, there are no stages, theories, holy truths, or teachings to get stuck in. At the same time, be warned not to get stuck in the experience of oneness. We also need to be aware of "the many"—the relative world of differences that is not other than essential nature manifesting moment by moment with a thousand different faces. There is no holy or unholy. There is only the one manifesting in "just this."

Marriage is neither holy nor unholy. It is just two human beings and the way they relate to one another in each moment. Along with stages are no stages—"just this." Each stage contains the other stages. The beginning romance stage of a relationship also includes conflict and mature love. Young love radiates out to open the hearts of others and touch them with new hope. In the last stage, a couple still experiences romance, conflict continues, and a mature love grows to inspire those that long for lasting love.

In relationships, as well as in spiritual development, sometimes insight grows and matures gradually, and sometimes it comes in sudden leaps that transform your life in unexpected ways. You light up the night sky like a sudden flash of lightning.

Wake up and experience your life this moment! Without thought, without separation, "What is it?" See for yourself! You don't need someone else's answer. If you do this and do not regress into thought, memory, or analysis, it is possible to see something new. Each moment it is possible to let go of the past and wake up to that which is new, fresh, vital, and sensitive. Your life and your relationship, this very moment, are full of unlimited possibilities. You and your partner can lead a creative and dynamic life together.

Creative energy is abundant and available when you open to your unbounded potential. With this insight comes the responsibility to respond, living your life fully and creatively. In our zendo at home, we have a large calligraphy by Yasutani Roshi that says:

> The meaning of Roshi coming from the West becomes clear.
> Palm to forehead.
> The essence of Zen takes root in another garden.
> A tree with white flowers blooms all on its own.

Early teachers who first brought Zen from Japan to America were pioneers. Although they brought the essence of Zen, they did not know what shape it would take as it took root in a new garden. Palm to forehead, with a look of surprise and amazement, we watch it blossom all on its own before our very eyes. As Zen wisdom grows in America, it enriches and is enriched by psychology, science, democracy, egalitarianism, and the religious traditions common in our culture. As Zen cross-pollinates with these other worldviews and traditions, its essence remains the same, but its form is new. This new flower not only adorns the altars of monasteries in America, it also adorns the homes and hearts of individuals and couples practicing Zen in the midst of ordinary everyday lives. Its beauty and fragrance have the potential to inspire us, in the zendo, in the kitchen, in the bedroom, in the workplace, and wherever we are on the spiritual path.

Relationships too are like this. As Zen comes West, it is becoming clear that the new pioneers are couples on the spiritual path. As the essence of Zen takes root in relationships, intimate partnerships are enriched, and also Zen is enriched and blossoms in a new way.

Whatever our spiritual path may be, our challenge as couples is to wake up moment by moment and create a life together that knows no limits. Cultivating love in your primary relationship is a spiritual practice and the work of a lifetime. In intimate partnership may we all learn to love and be loved fully and completely.

NOTES

AN INTIMATE JOURNEY

p. 3   The phrase "partners in life and wisdom" is adapted from a poem by the Cherokee/Appalachian writer Marilou Awiatka.

p. 3   The story about Liangshan and Guanzhi is adapted from Case 43 in *The Record of Transmitting the Light* translated by Francis Cook.

p. 4   The story about Fayan and Guichen is adapted from Katsuki Sekida's commentary on Case 26 of *The Gateless Gate*.

p. 5   The story about Buddha's enlightenment is adapted from Case 1 of *The Record of Transmitting the Light* translated by Francis Cook.

EXPANDING YOUR HEART

p. 6   The verse "The deep, subtle secret..." is adapted from *The Record of Transmitting the Light* translated by Francis Cook, p. 238.

p. 6   The quote by Dogen is from *The Wholehearted Way* translated by Shohaku Okumura and Taigen Daniel Leighton, p. 19.

p. 7   The story about Xuefeng is adapted from Case 5 in *The Blue Cliff Record* translated by Katsuki Sekida.

BEING A COMPANION

p. 11   The koan about a narrow mountain path is from *Miscellaneous Koans* by Toni Packer.

p. 11   The story about Dongshan and Nanquan is adapted from *The Record of Transmitting the Light* translated by Francis Cook, p. 194.

PARTNER AS TEACHER

p. 16   The story about Mazu and Huairang is adapted from *Three Pillars of Zen* by Philip Kapleau, p. 24.

p. 17   "I walk in beauty..." is from a Navajo song by Arliene Nofchissey.

p. 18   The quote by Dogen is adapted from *Sounds of Valley Streams* translated by Francis Cook, p. 66.

ON THE CUTTING EDGE

p. 26   "Who comes to commend me..." is from the poem *Cold Mountain* translated by Burton Watson, p. 29.

THIS MOMENT TOGETHER

p. 30   The story about the sixteen bodhisattvas is adapted from Case 78 in *The Blue Cliff Record* translated by Katsuki Sekida.

KNOWING YOURSELF AND NO-SELF

p. 37   The story about Guizong and Fayan is adapted from Case 7 in *The Blue Cliff Record* translated by Katsuki Sekida.

BOUNDARIES AND NO BOUNDARIES

p. 44   The verse "House demolished..." is from *The Record of Transmitting the Light* translated by Francis Cook, p. 50.

p. 45   The quote by Robert Frost is from his poem "Mending Wall."

NOT ONE, NOT TWO

p. 48   "Form is precisely emptiness..." is from "The Heart Sutra" from the *Zen Peacemaker Order Service Book*.

EVERYTHING CHANGES

p. 52   The story about Damei and Mazu is adapted from Cases 30 and 33 of *The Gateless Gate* translated by Koun Yamada.

RELATIONSHIP IS NOT A THING

p. 62   The quote by Keizan is adapted from *The Record of Transmitting the Light* translated by Francis Cook, p. 236.

p. 63   The story about Zhaozhau is adapted from Case 1 in *The Gateless Gate* translated by Koun Yamada.

p. 66   "Body is lost!..." is from a verse in Case 1 of *The Gateless Gate* translated by Koun Yamada.

ACCEPTING YOURSELF AND YOUR PARTNER

p. 71　"Just as I Am" is a hymn by Charlotte Elliott.

p. 73　"Every day is a good day" is from Case 6 in *The Blue Cliff Record* translated by Katsuki Sekida.

p. 73　The quote by Elizabeth Berg is from her novel *Talk Before Sleep*, p. 132.

p. 75　The quote by Walt Whitman is from his poem "Song of Myself."

FREEDOM IN RELATIONSHIP

p. 77　The quote by Yamada Roshi is from his commentary on *The Gateless Gate*, p. 85.

p. 78　The verse, "When a bird flies..." is from *The Record of Transmitting the Light* translated by Francis Cook.

p. 80　The story about Jianzhi is from Case 32 in *The Record of Transmitting the Light* translated by Francis Cook.

GIVING AND RECEIVING

p. 85　Guest and host are discussed in *The Secret of the Golden Flower* translated by Thomas Cleary, p. 143–146.

DARKNESS AND LIGHT

p. 87　"Light is also darkness..." is from "The Identity of Relative and Absolute" from the Zen Peacemaker Order Service Book.

RESPECTING EACH OTHER

p. 90　The phrase "raising the Bodhi mind" is from the "Gate of Sweet Nectar" from the *Zen Peacemaker Order Service Book.*

BEING TOGETHER

p. 94　The quote by Hongzhi is from *Cultivating the Empty Field* translated by Taigen Daniel Leighton and Yi Wu.

COMMUNICATION BEYOND SPEECH AND SILENCE

p. 107　The story about Buddha and Mahakashyapa is adapted from Case 2 in *The Record of Transmitting the Light* translated by Francis Cook.

p. 108　The verse "If you meet a swordsman..." is from *The Gateless Gate* translated by Koun Yamada, p. 164.

p. 109   The story about the non-Buddhist is adapted from Case 45 in *The Record of Transmitting the Light* translated by Francis Cook.

DISAGREEING WITHOUT DIVISION

p. 111   The story about Nanquan is adapted from Case 14 in *The Gateless Gate* translated by Koun Yamada.

p. 112   The verse "Thoughtless the monks of both halls..." is from *The Blue Cliff Record* translated by Katsuki Sekida, p. 319.

p. 113   "If there is a trace..." is from the poem "Affirming Faith in Mind" by the sixth century Chinese Zen Master Sengcan.

p. 115   The story about Ananda and Mahakashyapa is adapted from Case 22 in *The Gateless Gate* translated by Koun Yamada.

NO BLAMING

p. 118   The story about Qiannu and Wangzhou is adapted from Case 35 in *The Gateless Gate* translated by Koun Yamada.

p. 120   "The relative fits the Absolute..." is from "The Identity of Relative and Absolute" from the *Zen Peacemaker Order Service Book*.

p. 121   The verse "Don't draw another's bow..." is from *The Gateless Gate* translated by Koun Yamada.

NOT JUDGING OR CRITICIZING

p. 122   The story about Fayan is adapted from Case 26 in *The Gateless Gate* translated by Koun Yamada.

LOVEMAKING

p. 128   "The whole body..." is from Case 89 in *The Blue Cliff Record* translated by Katsuki Sekida.

p. 128   The phrase "love's body" is from the book *Love's Body* by Norman O. Brown.

p. 129   The story about Dogen and Rujing is adapted from Case 52 in *The Record of Transmitting the Light* translated by Francis Cook.

GRATITUDE AND GENEROSITY

p. 134   The story about Qingshui and Caoshan is adapted from Case 10 in *The Gateless Gate* translated by Koun Yamada.

p. 135   "For the wonders that astound us…" is a verse from "Hymn for the Fruits of Creation" by Fred Pratt Green.

TAKING TURNS

p. 138   The koan about Zhaozhau's Three Turning Words is from Case 96 in *The Blue Cliff Record* translated by Katsuki Sekida.

NURTURING CHILDREN

p. 141   The story about Yunmen is adapted from Case 16 in *Zen Comments on the Mumonkan* by Zenkei Shibayama.

MAKING A LIVING

p. 144   Information about Baizhang is from *The Golden Age of Zen* by John C. H. Wu, p. 82–85.

WORK PRACTICE AT HOME: SHARING HOUSEHOLD CHORES

p. 151   The story about Rujing is adapted from Case 51 in *The Record of Transmitting the Light* translated by Francis Cook.

HOME AS SACRED SPACE

p. 153   The story about Bodhidharma is adapted from Case 41 in *The Gateless Gate* translated by Koun Yamada.

BEFORE LOVE ARRIVES

p. 158   The story about Jingquin is adapted from Case 16 in *The Blue Cliff Record* translated by Katsuki Sekida.

IS THIS IT?

p. 161   "Love is always patient…" is from First Corinthians 13:4 in *The Jerusalem Bible*.

p. 163   The quote by Robert Frost is from his poem "The Road Not Taken."

p. 164   "If you do not see the Way…" is from "The Identity of Relative and Absolute" from the *Zen Peacemaker Order Service Book*.

ENDING RELATIONSHIPS

p. 165   The story about the man in the tree is adapted from Case 5 in *The Gateless Gate* translated by Koun Yamada.

IN GOOD TIMES AND BAD

p. 177   The story about Dongshan is adapted from Case 43 in *The Blue Cliff Record* translated by Katsuki Sekida.

p. 179   The story about Mazu is adapted from Case 3 in *The Blue Cliff Record* translated by Katsuki Sekida.

FOR AS LONG AS WE BOTH SHALL LIVE

p. 184   "Jesus wept." is from John 11:36 in *The Jerusalem Bible*.

p. 185   The story about Suzong and Huizhong is adapted from Case 18 in *The Blue Cliff Record* translated by Katsuki Sekida.

p. 187   The story about Zhaozhou is adapted from Case 37 in *The Gateless Gate* translated by Koun Yamada.

EVERYTHING IS INTERCONNECTED

p. 191   The question asked by Songyuan is from Koun Yamada's commentary on Case 20 in *The Gateless Gate*, p. 99.

p. 192   "Our human calling is to relate…" is translated from a Taize song called "Confitemini Domino" by J. Berthier.

PULLING TOGETHER

p. 193   The koan about the hundred foot pole is adapted from Case 46 in *The Gateless Gate* translated by Koun Yamada.

p. 195   The story about Lianhua is adapted from Case 25 in *The Blue Cliff Record* translated by Katsuki Sekida.

SERVANT OF THE SERVANT

p. 198   The story about Chuhui Zhenji is adapted from *The Golden Age of Zen* by John C. Wu, p. 185.

p. 199   The question asked by Wuzu is from Case 45 in *The Gateless Gate* translated by Koun Yamada.

OCEAN OF COMPASSION

p. 201   The quote by Wendy Egyoku Nakao is from *Zen Flashes*, p. 10.

CO-CREATING UNLIMITED POSSIBILITIES

p. 204   Evelyn Duvall's stages of family development are from her classic text *Family Development*.

p. 205   The story about Qingyuan is adapted from Case 35 in *The Record of Transmitting the Light* translated by Francis Cook.

REFERENCES

Marilou Awiatka, "Selu" (Appalachian Regional Studies Center, Radford University, Radford, VA, photocopy).

Elizabeth Berg, *Talk Before Sleep*. (New York: Random House, 1994).

J. Berthier, "Confitemini Domino." (Chicago: GIA Publications, Inc.).

Norman O. Brown, *Love's Body*. (New York: Random House, 1966).

Thomas Cleary, trans., *The Secret of the Golden Flower: The Classic Chinese Book of Life*. (San Francisco: Harper, 1991).

Francis Cook, trans., *The Record of Transmitting the Light: Zen Master Keizan's Denkoroku*. (Boston: Wisdom Publications, 2003).

Francis Cook, trans., *Sounds of Valley Streams*. (Albany: State University of New York, 1989).

Evelyn Duvall, *Family Development*. (Philadelphia: Lippincott, 1971).

Robert Frost, *The Poetry of Robert Frost*. (New York: Henry Holt, 1969).

Fred Pratt Green, "Hymn for the Fruits of Creation." (Hope Publishing Co., 1970).

Philip Kapleau, *Three Pillars of Zen: Teaching, Practice, and Enlightenment*. (New York: Anchor, 1989).

Taigen Daniel Leighton & Yi Wu, trans., *Cultivating the Empty Field: The Silent Illumination of Zen Master Hongzhi*. (San Francisco: North Point Press, 1991).

Wendy Egyoku Nakao, *Zen Flashes*. (Zen Center of Los Angeles, 923 S. Normandie Ave., Los Angeles, CA 90006, 2003).

Arliene Nofchissey, "I Walk in Beauty" (Phoenix, AZ: Canyon Records Productions, Inc.).

Shohaku Okumura & Taigen Daniel Leighton, trans., *The Wholehearted Way.* (Boston: Tuttle, 1997).

Toni Packer, *Miscellaneous Koans* (Rochester, NY: Genesee Valley Zen Center, 1983).

Katsuki Sekida, *Two Zen Classics: Mumonkan & Hekiganroku.* (New York: Weatherhill, 1977).

Zenkei Shibayama, *Zen Comments on the Mumonkan.* (New York: Harper & Row, 1974).

Chogyam Trungpa, *Cutting Through Spiritual Materialism.* (Boston: Shambhala, 2002).

Burton Watson, trans., *Cold Mountain.* (Boston: Shambhala, 1992).

Norman Weddell, trans., *The Unborn: The Life and Teachings of Zen Master Bankei.* (New York: North Point Press, 2000)

Walt Whitman, *Leaves of Grass.* (New York: Random House, 1950/1855).

John C. H. Wu, *The Golden Age of Zen.* (New York: Doubleday, 1996).

Koun Yamada, *Gateless Gate.* (Tucson: University of Arizona Press, 1990).

Zen Peacemaker Order Service Book. (Peacemaker Circle International, Inc., 177 Ripley Road, Montague, MA 01351, 1997).

PERMISSIONS

INDEX

ABOUT THE AUTHORS

Photo by Lora Gordon

ELLEN BIRX has a Ph.D. in psychiatric nursing and for the past twenty years has been a professor at Radford University. She is a Zen teacher and the author of *Healing Zen*. CHARLES BIRX, also a Zen teacher, is retired from a career as a reading specialist and adjunct assistant professor in the College of Education and Human Development at Radford University. The Birxes are cofounders of New River Zen Community (www.newriverzen.org). They have been married for thirty-seven years and live together in Radford, Virginia.

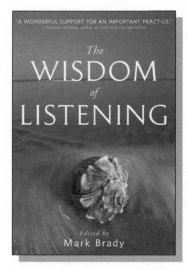

THE WISDOM OF LISTENING
Edited by Mark Brady
320 pages, ISBN 0-86171-355-9, $16.95

"In this thoughtful anthology, eighteen contemporary spiritual teachers explore the transformative effects, and the difficulties, of skillful listening and suggest ways in which becoming someone who listens mindfully, with focused attention, can improve relationships. Free of religious dogma and self-help cliches, the essays are inspiring, intelligent, and accessible."—*SpaFinder*

"Brady has put together a very helpful anthology of 19 essays with sections on the promise, the practice, and the power of listening. Among the contributors are spiritual teacher Ram Dass; Marshall Rosenberg, founder of the Center for Nonviolent Communication; Anne Simpkinson, an editor for *Prevention* magazine; Kathleen Dowling Singh, a therapist and workshop leader; and Rodney Smith, director of the Hospice of Seattle. Using a variety of terms to describe this type of communion, they offer suggestions, perspectives, and practices that will reinforce your intentions to be a good listener."—*Spirituality and Health*

"Bravo! As I read *The Wisdom of Listening*, I kept marking passages and copying bits out to send to friends—a good sign! This book is a treasure chest of useful and meaningful practices and ideas."—James Fadiman, Ph.D. Author, *The Other Side of Haight*

MINDFULNESS YOGA:
The Awakened Union of Breath, Body, and Mind
Frank Jude Boccio
Foreword by Georg Feuerstein
320 pages, 100 photos,
ISBN 0-86171-335-4, $19.95

An entirely new integration of yoga and meditation! Whether you're a beginner or have been practicing for years, *Mindfulness Yoga* is for you. Easy-to-follow sequences are laid out with over 100 accompanying photos in this groundbreaking presentation of mindfulness meditation and yoga. Special lay-flat binding makes this book even more useful as a practice aid.

"*Mindfulness Yoga* should be read by *every* aspiring Yoga practitioner."
—Georg Feuerstein, author of *The Yoga Tradition*

"EDITOR'S CHOICE! No one has offered a successful book-length discourse fully integrating Buddhist meditation and yoga until Frank Jude Boccio came along."—*Yoga Journal*

"I highly recommend this book. There is something here for everyone, from beginning students to more advanced practitioners alike. And the sections on practice are designed—refreshingly—for real human beings! Bravo!"—Stephen Cope, psychotherapist, senior Kripalu Yoga teacher, and author of *Yoga and the Quest for the True Self*

"It's about time somebody wrote this!"—Jon Kabat-Zinn, author of *Wherever You Go, There You Are* and *Coming to Our Senses*

MEDITATION FOR LIFE
Martine Batchelor
Photographs by Stephen Batchelor
168 pages, ISBN 0-86171-320-8, $22.95

"Among today's steady stream of new books on Buddhist meditation, most are easy to ignore. This one isn't. It offers simple, concrete instructions in meditation and the photographs are delicious eye-candy. Author Martine Batchelor spent ten years in a Korean monastery and presumably knows a lotus position when she sees one—she also has a sense of humor."—*Psychology Today*

"A good place to start is with *Meditation for Life*. A thoughtful, thorough book."—*Spafinder*

LIVING ZEN, LOVING GOD
Ruben L.F. Habito
Foreword by John Keenan, co-editor of
Beside Still Waters
160 pages, ISBN 0-86171-383-4, $14.95

"A pioneering example of what I call *interspirituality:* the experiential exploration of another tradition while remaining committed to one's home tradition. Finding the common ground between Christianity and Zen in contemplative practice, he also discovered what so many others have: plunging into the depth of another tradition sheds fresh light on one's faith in the home tradition, and does so in a positive way, consonant with one's faith. This is a very valuable book."—Brother Wayne Teasdale, author of *The Mystic Heart*

ZEN MEDITATION IN PLAIN ENGLISH

John Daishin Buksbazen
Foreword by Peter Matthiessen
128 pages, ISBN 0-86171-316-8, $12.95

"Buksbazen offers practical and down-to-earth advice about the specifics of Zen meditation: how and when to breathe; what to think about. This is a fine introduction to Zen meditation practice, grounded in tradition yet adapted to contemporary life."
—*Publishers Weekly*

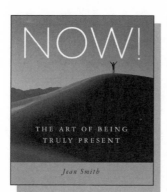

NOW!

The Art of Being Truly Present
Jean Smith
144 pages with French flaps,
ISBN 0-86171-480-6, $14.00

"In this timely paperback, the author elucidates the bounties of mindfulness and meditation. On each left-hand page, you will find a brief commentary on a subject that is a natural part of daily living; these are intended to be used for pondering, journaling, or discussion in small groups. On the opposite page, you will find invocations [that function as] verses for reflection. These are designed to bring the practice of mindfulness to every moment of existence so that nothing is slighted or overlooked. The book is organized into segments on presence of spirit, of heart, of mind, of conduct, in relationship, and in the world. These reflections and invocations can bring us to a fresh appreciation of being present."—*Spirituality and Health*

ABOUT WISDOM

W ISDOM PUBLICATIONS, a nonprofit publisher, is dedicated to making available authentic Buddhist works for the benefit of all. We publish translations of the sutras and tantras, commentaries and teachings of past and contemporary Buddhist masters, and original works by the world's leading Buddhist scholars. We publish our titles with the appreciation of Buddhism as a living philosophy and with the special commitment to preserve and transmit important works from all the major Buddhist traditions.

To learn more about Wisdom, or to browse books online, visit our website at wisdompubs.org. You may request a copy of our mail-order catalog online or by writing to:

Wisdom Publications
199 Elm Street
Somerville, Massachusetts 02144 USA
Telephone: (617) 776-7416
Fax: (617) 776-7841
Email: info@wisdompubs.org
www.wisdompubs.org

The Wisdom Trust

As a nonprofit publisher, Wisdom is dedicated to the publication of fine Dharma books for the benefit of all sentient beings and dependent upon the kindness and generosity of sponsors in order to do so. If you would like to make a donation to Wisdom, please do so through our Somerville office. If you would like to sponsor the publication of a book, please write or email us at the address above.

Thank you.

Wisdom is a nonprofit, charitable 501(c)(3) organization affiliated with the Foundation for the Preservation of the Mahayana Tradition (FPMT).